History & Guide
WIGAN

History & Guide
WIGAN

John Hannavy

First published 2003

Reprinted in 2008 by The History Press

The History Press
The Mill, Brimscombe Port
Stroud, Gloucestershire Gl 5 2q G
www.thehistorypress.co.uk

Reprinted 2013

© John Hannavy, 2003

The right of John Hannavy to be identified as the Author
of this work has been asserted by him in accordance with the
Copyrights, Designs and Patents Act 1988.

All rights reserved. No part of this book may be reprinted
or reproduced or utilised in any form or by any electronic,
mechanical or other means, now known or hereafter invented,
including photocopying and recording, or in any information
storage or retrieval system, without the permission in writing
from the Publishers.

British library Cataloguing in Publication Data.
A catalogue record for this book is available from the British library.

ISBN 978 0 7524 3099 7

Typesetting and origination by
Tempus Publishing.
Printed and bound by TJ International Ltd, Padstow, Cornwall

Contents

	Introduction	6
1	Origins and Early History	8
2	The Ancient and Loyal Borough	18
3	Haigh Hall – History and Legend	30
4	Tudor and Elizabethan Wigan and Beyond	38
5	Wigan During the Civil War	44
6	The Eighteenth-Century Industrial Town	57
7	Victorian Wigan: Cotton, Coal and Railways	67
8	Wigan in the Twentieth Century	78
9	Famous Wigan, Famous Wiganers	93
	Walking Tour 1: Wigan Town Centre	97
	Walking Tour 2: Wigan Pier	113
	Bibliography	127
	Acknowledgements	128

Introduction

Sitting down five years ago to start writing my ninth book on Wigan in twenty-five years, was, in some respects, daunting. To present a fresh look at the town's history was a challenge but, luckily, so much interesting material about Wigan still remains to be discovered and shared. New pictures are constantly being discovered – and several of them appear here, I believe, for the first time in print.

I was helped, too, by the format of the series into which this book fits, giving me the opportunity to guide you, the reader, round some of the familiar and perhaps some unfamiliar places in Wigan.

Of course, when dealing with a factual history, much of the material contained in the following pages was unearthed and researched during preparation for my 1990 book *Historic Wigan*, now long out of print.

It is nearly forty years since I first came to live in the town after being appointed to my first teaching post at what was then Wigan & District Mining & Technical College, now Wigan & Leigh College. So much has changed since then – the policeman who used to direct at the top of Library Street has been gone for more than a generation, Commercial Yard was buried beneath the Wigan Centre (now the Marketgate Shopping Centre) almost as long ago, and the Market Square Bus Station and Whelans Supermarket have long since been replaced by the Galleries. The building in which I used to teach has been the Town Hall for many years, and the once-magnificent Ritz cinema and theatre, where Buddy Holly and later the Beatles once performed, has been demolished, and Station Road on which it stood is now lost beneath the new Royal Arcade Shopping Centre. In the opening years of the 21st century with shopping increasingly moving out of town to the Robin Park development, the Royal Arcade project is a brave attempt to redress the balance and bring shoppers back into the town centre in large numbers. In the short term, though, it has created swathes of empty shops in Standishgate and in the Galleries as big stores move into the new development. The number of large empty stores in the town centre is a worrying footnote to the new development.

It is a poignant reminder of how times have changed in the last three decades to remember that traffic was relatively light in the 1970s, and Library Street, Wallgate, Market Street and Standishgate were all open to two-way traffic, there was no ring road, and bus lanes were a thing of the future. Buses were all owned by the corporation, and they were burgundy and white, as had been tram cars and trolley buses before them. Five years

Wigan Market Place in the late eighteenth century, from a contemporary engraving. Thomas Whitehouse, a nineteenth-century liquor merchant included a watercolour based on this engraving in his 1830 manuscript history of the town.

ago, when writing this book, it was pleasantly nostalgic to see a FirstBus double-decker driving around in the old Corporation colours – but that too is now nothing more than a memory.

Perhaps the most remarkable transformation in my time in Wigan has been the reversal of the fortunes of the pier and the canal basin. When I arrived here in 1969, Wigan Pier was a joke appreciated by few if anyone within the town. It was seen as a major civic embarrassment, but with its re-emergence in the mid 1980s as an award-winning contribution to the late twentieth century heritage cult, the last laugh was very definitely enjoyed by Wiganers who found a new pride in their history and culture. It is to be hoped that the development of the area surrounding the pier as a new cultural quarter will add further vigour to this part of town.

The greatest changes have taken longer to come about, as a look at century-old photographs and postcards reminds us. It makes you wonder just what the town will look like in thirty years' time or even a century's time.

A generation of Wiganers has come and gone since I wrote my first book on the town thirty years ago, and this 'Wigan History & Guide' will be my last, as I too have now moved away. I will, however, always retain a soft spot for one of the country's most enigmatic towns – a town which has consistently re-invented itself over the centuries and which, doubtless, will continue to evolve and change in years to come.

John Hannavy,
Great Cheverell, Wiltshire,
Spring 2008

CHAPTER 1
Origins and Early History

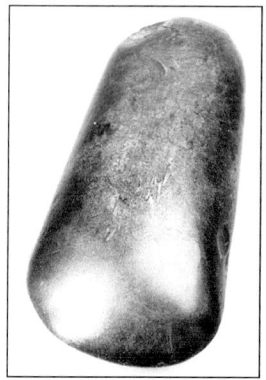

A Neolithic axehead, now in the Wigan Heritage Service Collection.

While Wigan Pier is undoubtedly responsible for the town's enduring fame, it is to the River Douglas that the town owes its existence. It would have been the pure, fresh and abundant waters of the Dhu Glas – the Black River – which attracted the original settlers thousands of years ago to the hillside site by a bend in the river.

It was by that same river that the Romans established their settlement and, one thousand years later it was the Douglas which initially brought the town prosperity by powering the first corn mills. Later still, before coal changed everything, it was the fast-running Douglas which powered the first cotton mills.

After centuries of appalling pollution, the river, which flows down to the town from Rivington Moor before turning north west to meet the River Ribble, is now being slowly but surely cleaned up.

The name 'Wigan' is a curious one, and its roots are uncertain. It is not clear when the town became known as Wigan, and although several suggestions as to its roots have been made over the years, all are conjecture, and not one of them has that unequivocal air of certainty about it.

David Sinclair, writing in his 1882 *History of Wigan* quotes an eighteenth-century writer, Bailey, who suggested the origin of the name

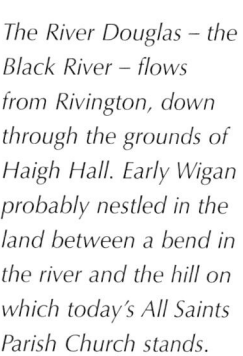

The River Douglas – the Black River – flows from Rivington, down through the grounds of Haigh Hall. Early Wigan probably nestled in the land between a bend in the river and the hill on which today's All Saints Parish Church stands.

might have been Pibiggin, a word with possible Roman roots. A possible meaning, according to Bailey, might be 'sacred buildings'. His theory requires that the Latinised name was later corrupted by the Anglo-Saxons to Wibiggin, Wiggin and eventually Wigan! There is, however, little evidence of an etymological timeline which might substantiate such a derivation

Sinclair also acknowledged the currency of several alternative suggestions, one of which was built around the fact that the wiggin tree was a commonly used name for the ash tree, and that two trees – perhaps ash trees – featured in the town's ancient coat of arms. Other sources – including the Encylcopaedia Britannica – suggest Wygan, or Wigham as the original name, and Sinclair also refers to Wigham as a possible root which, he believed, might mean 'fighting place' or 'fighting town'. It is more likely that the name has its origins in a Brigantian family name. Whatever the root, there is certainly no connection between any of them and Coccium, the name of the Roman camp or settlement which probably occupied land adjacent to the River Douglas.

Many sources seem to point to the Roman arrival by the banks of the Douglas as the beginnings of the town of Wigan itself. But archaeological evidence, albeit fragmentary, does suggest an earlier occupation.

The pre-Roman history of the town, unsurprisingly, is even more obscure than the derivation of the name. Archaeological evidence unearthed over the years points to the site having been occupied during successive ages over the past two millennia but, as those civilisations did not keep written records, the exact location, extent and nature of their settlements is unknown.

A variety of artifacts from early civilisations has survived – including finely made axe-heads, arrow heads and other items.

There is further confusion over the exact nature of the Roman presence – was it a military camp alone, or was there a civilian settlement associated with it – neither option can be confirmed or denied.

Indeed, for a long time, there was doubt over whether or not Wigan was actually the site of the Roman 'Coccium' – with Blackrod and Standish being suggested as possible alternatives.

That was finally settled some twenty years ago, when the Greater Manchester Archaeological Unit discovered traces of first- and second-century buildings on the site of the Wiend Centre. Given the discovery of remains of the same period during early nineteenth-century work constructing the town's gas works, there clearly was quite a sizeable settlement – or settlements – of some kind. Perhaps a Roman military station and a Brigantian civilian settlement existed side by side.

As with the town's name, the Roman name presents problems. While Wigan is now generally accepted as the site of the settlement, *Coccium*

Two coins from the reign of the Emperor Antoninus, from the collection of Roman coins discovered at the Boar's Head in the 1920s. The collection contained coins from the entire period of the Roman occupation of the town, suggesting the Boar's Head might have been the site of a signal station, or mile post on the road north.

An ancient Roman altar was discovered during an eighteenth-century restoration of the Parish Church. It was originally set into the outside wall of the tower but, a century later during a further restoration, it was relocated to a window recess inside the tower where it remains to this day.

The ceilings in the Georgian wing of the now-demolished Standish Hall celebrated the town's Roman connections. In the drawing room, the plaster profile of a Roman Emperor – probably Hadrian – featured in the central ceiling pane, while centurions featured in the surrounding plasterwork.

is not an obviously Roman word. The Celtic word 'coccion' of 'cochion' – believed to have meant 'red' is close enough to *Coccium* to be a possible root. Given the predominance of red sand and red clay in the neighbourhood, a settlement on the 'red land' or 'red hill' might suggest a Brigantian settlement on the site long before Roman occupation. *Coccium*, as the name of the Roman settlement, could therefore be explained as a Latinisation of the Brigantian name.

Accepting that there was a Roman presence by the banks of the Douglas, we are no closer to defining it. It is described in encyclopaedias and histories variously as a fort, a post, a settlement and a town, and of

course its importance depends upon just which of those it was. While the Roman presence in or near the site of the modern town is beyond dispute, the sparcity of remains must point to it being less than a Roman town. A military station of some importance – at least towards the end of the Roman period – is the most likely theory, perhaps with a civilian presence alongside it, but not necessarily Roman. If there was pre-Roman occupation of the site, then the Roman garrison was probably established either alongside it, or in place of it. The remains which have been found were the marks in the ground left by wooden structures rather than stone, more in keeping with supply facilities than with a Roman town. Or they may have been remains of buildings associated with a civilian settlement adjacent to the military site.

The area around present-day Wigan was largely unknown to the Romans until at least half way through the first century AD. It was only after Agricola moved further north towards the end of the first century that civilian settlements started to be established. After all, the great Roman cities of York (*Eboracum*) and Chester (*Deva*) only date from that period. It was also then that Roman roads were developed and consolidated, but those first roads came nowhere near Wigan.

The two original main roads north from *Deva* led directly to *Mamucium* (present-day Manchester) and *Bremetennacum* (Ribchester). It was the new road north to Lancaster – through Wilderspool and Walton-de-Dale – which placed *Coccium* on the Roman map, but while evidence of civilian occupation has been found elsewhere on the route, the true purpose of *Coccium* has never been clarified.

Given the importance of Winwick in pre-Roman times, the new road may well have been built over an existing track leading to Brigantian settlements – which would explain its meandering route, quite different from the Roman norm of building straight roads which were more direct and easier to defend.

Coccium's importance was further enhanced in the second century when another road was laid from *Mamucium* to meet the north-south road at the ford on the River Douglas. The Romans can never have found the movement of troops and supplies up to cross the River at *Bremetennacum* easy, and the road to Lancaster via *Coccium* offered an easier passage. The building of twenty miles of new road to *Coccium* would have made the entire journey less physically demanding, and coincides with the building of Hadrian's Wall, when the movement of huge convoys of troops, labourers and supplies was of paramount importance. The straight line of the road suggests that this route was an entirely Roman construction.

Coccium now sat at an important and significant junction on the Roman road network, and it is not unreasonable to assume that at that time it became more than just a fort.

Three coins from the reign of the Emperor Septimus Severus, also from the collection of Roman coins discovered at the Boar's Head in the 1920s. Septimus Severus was Emperor from AD 193 until 211, and came to Britain to lead campaigns against the Picts between AD 208-209.

There is very little surviving evidence of the routes taken by these two roads, but records from the nineteenth century show that parts of the east-west road were evident at that time passing through Amberswood Common. Examination of modern maps offers an insight into their possible route into today's town.

We know that the road from Manchester was built across open ground, whereas the road up from Wilderspool probably largely followed the meandering line of an existing track (the route taken by the present-day A49) arriving somewhere around the foot of Wallgate. As it approached *Coccium*, the Romans would have insisted that the route was straight and easy to defend. So the present-day twists and turns as the A49 approaches the town are probably much later deviations from the Roman line.

The roads would have been paved, about twelve metres wide, with clear land either side – no bushes or trees to offer protection to would-be attackers. Records show that traces of the paving was also discovered in the first half of the nineteenth century during the construction of the main west coast railway line through the town.

Interestingly, the line of Wallgate, if continued straight from the railway bridge at North Western station, would meet the projected line of the east-west road well to the south east of the present town centre. If the routes were as described, work on the railway would indeed have crossed the line of the north-south Roman road.

Nineteenth century historians traced the line of that east-west road through Hindley, crossing the Douglas at the ford which used to be located near the bottom of Millgate. If those two routes are correct, then the roads would intersect somewhere well south of today's Market Place

The area of the town bounded by Darlington Street, Chapel Lane, Millgate, the Inner Ring Road and the River Douglas may mark out the site of the Roman station of Coccium.

The Boars Head Inn – the second oldest pub in England – seen here in a 1905 postcard, has been a coaching inn since the thirteenth century. Beneath it, cells once held prisoners on their way to execution in Lancaster Castle. It was near the Boars Head that the hoard of Roman coins was discovered in the 1920s.

– probably near the International Pool – and that intersection might have marked one corner of the Roman settlement.

By the middle of the second century, the Roman front line was between the rivers Forth and Clyde, leaving *Coccium* in an area of relative peace and stability, but there is no evidence of any great civilian development in the area. There is no evidence of villa development north of Chester, and no evidence that the Romans farmed the lands between *Coccium* and the sea. Had there been such developments, archaeological evidence would have survived. The absence of such evidence in the plains between *Coccium* and the sea underlines the essentially military nature of places like *Coccium*.

The finds to date seem to bear that out – the coins discovered are generally no later than the late second or early-third century, perhaps implying that when the strategic importance of the site waned, the Romans moved out.

The overwhelming picture, therefore, is of a military presence, perhaps with an adjacent Romanised-Brigantian settlement, the local peoples being increasingly influenced by Roman standards of civilisation.

But as the Roman presence was essentially military, there was no great dawning of a Rome-inspired enlightenment amongst the local peoples. That was reserved for the Romano-British further south. They may have been some inter-marriage between the garrison and the locals, but it is unlikely to have been widespread.

There was, however, a considerable amount of industrial development around the garrison posts – presumably to meet the needs of the troops. Evidence of ceramic manufacture, glass making and metal working has been found at both Wilderspool and Stockton Heath – but not yet in the area surrounding *Coccium*. Of course, the extensive eighteenth- and nineteenth-century developments by the river near Darlington Street and Chapel lane may have destroyed that!

As Rome gradually withdrew from Britain, sites like *Coccium* were just abandoned – and unless they left a few stone foundations underpinning their wooden military buildings, they may have left little trace of their occupation behind them. Thus nineteenth-century romantic accounts of the Romans leaving a deserted town to be taken over by the Anglo-Saxons have no basis whatsoever.

The Romans withdrew from Britain over a period of several years in the early fifth century, withdrawing completely by AD 430.

What happened to *Coccium*, or any civilian settlement adjacent to it, in the years immediately following the Romans leaving, we do not know. It is unlikely that the area was immediately taken over by the *Anglii*, as records elsewhere suggest that they first crossed the Pennines, further south, no earlier than the late-sixth century.

They were farmers and valley-dwellers, and when they did arrive, it is reasonable to presume that they organised agriculture in the area between the Pennines and the sea. It follows, therefore, that their influence on the economy of the Wigan area would have immediately become of greater significance than the Romans, providing work on the lands, albeit as serfs, for the indigenous local community.

A plausible scenario would see the civilian settlement of Wigan – which had survived alongside the Roman station of *Coccium* – reassert its primacy and start to develop.

Further south the departure of the Romans resulted in a loss of the cultural and civilising influences they had brought with them, but further north, where their influence was largely military, there had never been any such benefit for the local communities. With the Romans gone, there was a move away from written records further south, but again that was of marginal significance in the north west.

By all accounts, the arrival of the *Angles* was a tumultuous event, but eventually a measure of peaceful coexistence was achieved. According to several (probably fanciful) accounts, Wigan emerged from this period as a fortified Anglo-Saxon town, complete with walls, but there is neither recorded nor archaeological evidence to support this. Indeed, little is known of Wigan's fortunes throughout the Dark Ages.

The Danish invasion in the late nineth century stopped well south of the town, so Wigan was spared that trauma – but in any case the sting had rather gone out of the Danish onslaught by the time they reached the site of present-day south Manchester.

It was not until the early tenth century that Wigan entered into a period of significant change. It was about then that an influx of Norse settlers appeared. This was not an invasion by the marauding Norse forces as has often been pictured. These 'invaders' were already well established in Ireland, and along the west coast of Scotland, and their move into

An ancient Celtic Cross discovered during one of the parish church's nineteenth-century restorations. It is now set into a wall inside the church. Its original location is unknown, as is its date.

Standishgate had been the main 'gata' or road north out of the town for more than a thousand years when it was pedestrianised in the 1980s. This view shows the street decorated for Christmas 1986 shortly after work on the paving of the pedestrian precinct had been completed. Its name is a direct link back to the Norse settlers in the tenth century.

the north-west of England was a gradual colonisation rather than an invasion. If their introduction was gradual, their impact was significant and enduring.

The Norse settlement was, initially, on the opposite side of the River Douglas to Wigan, and the name 'Scholes' is a reminder of that settlement. They also established a settlement at Skelmersdale.

It is assumed that intermarriage brought the Norse and British communities closer together, and it is known that Norse culture quickly dominated. Indeed Lancashire children were still being given Norse names well into the thirteenth century!

The layout of the streets radiating out from the old Wigan town centre – focused on Market Place – is almost certainly a legacy of the Norse influence. The Norse word for street – 'gata' – survives to this day in the early town's four prime streets – Standishgate, Wallgate, Millgate and Hallgate. Interestingly, some very early maps show Hallgate extending straight through the area occupied by today's Marketgate Shopping Centre, and meeting Wallgate, Standishgate and Millgate in a smaller open space near today's W.H.Smith's bookshop.

The Norse settlers, like their native Wigan neighbours, were Christian, so at least religious conflicts were not a problem. At the time of the arrival of the settlers, Wigan was still part of the ancient Kingdom of Northumbria, but by the second half of the tenth century, south Lancashire had been annexed by King Athelstan of Mercia. It appears not to have been officially incorporated into the kingdom, but kept as a royal property by the king.

1960s maisonettes in Scholes, with nineteenth-century terraced housing behind. It was in this area that the Norse settlement was established in the early tenth century.

The ancient cross base at the top of Standishgate, which has long been known locally as Mab's Cross, may date from as early as the eleventh or twelfth century.

South Lancashire was divided into six baronies or 'wapentakes' by Athelstan – Walintune (Warrington), Derbei (Derby), Salford, Blacheburn (Blackburn), Lailand (Leyland) and Neweton or Newton. Wigan was in the wapentake of Neweton, which may say something about the relative importance of the town when compared with Warrington, Salford, Blackburn and Leyland. Coupled with the total absence of any mention of the town in Anglo-Saxon times, and the idea of the walled town at the central of local life and industry becomes rather less substantial.

Further evidence – or further lack of evidence – comes from the fact that the Norman Domesday Book makes no mention of the town whatsoever. Wigan's importance clearly at that time, still lay in the future.

The baronies of Lancashire and Cheshire – wapentakes in Norse language by 'hundreds' in Norman parlance – occupy only about a page and a half in the Domesday book, and as in Norse times, it is the Barony of Newton which is mentioned, not the town of Wigan. And as Lancashire did not exist, Newton is included under Cheshire!

Under Norman rule, the former royal lands of the Mercian king were given to Roger de Poitou in 1072 or 1073, apparently as a reward for his loyalty during the invasion. Poitou divided his lands up generally in line with the Norse wapentakes, and the Newton lands were passed to Warinus Banastre who became Baron of Newton in the years immediately preceding the holding of the first great national census which culminated in the creation of the Domesday Book.

By the time of the census in 1086, Poitou had fallen out of favour with his king – and William himself had resumed nominal control of all six of the wapentakes, or hundreds.

Newton was recorded in the Domesday Book as by far the poorest of the six hundreds, with a value estimated at ten pounds and ten shillings. By comparison, Blackburn was valued at almost three times that figure.

So, as England prepared to enter the twelfth century, Wigan had yet to make its mark. It was at the time perhaps no more than a very small town surrounding a small stone church on the hill above the Black River.

It is all the more surprising, given its low profile, that at the dawn of the twelfth century, the township should, apparently, have been granted a degree of self-determination – which might be seen as having been quite disproportionate to its importance. But that may well be what happened.

Wiganers have often described their town as the oldest borough in what we now know as Lancashire – a claim based on a long-held belief that King Henry I, in a charter dated 1100, granted the town a measure of organisational independence. If there ever was such a charter, it is long lost! Indeed, its existence is only hinted at in a report to the College of

Heralds dated 1613, more than five hundred years after it was supposedly granted.

What may make a more plausible story would be something much less formal – a 'charter' or licence granted by the local Baron, allowing the inhabitants of the town a degree of self-determination. Such freedoms, while well short of the sort of municipal status a fully fledged royal charter later granted to the town, may well have acted as the trigger for a period of gradual but sustained growth, resulting almost a century and a half later in the royal charter from King Henry III, the 750th anniversary of which was celebrated in 1996.

The Lord of the Manor in twelfth-century England had immense power. He effectively exercised total control over the living and working conditions of those who resided on his land. He was landowner, employer, judge, jury and tax collector.

There can be little doubt that by the early years of the twelfth century, Wigan was becoming a local trading centre, with merchants either resident in the town, or bringing their wares in to sell at the local markets.

Given that emerging significance, and the growing prevalence of merchant fraternities or guilds throughout late eleventh-century England, the local landowner may well have had to concede that there was increasing business activity within the town over which he had no title. The logical thing to do – albeit rather ground-breaking in its day – would have been to recognise that limited independence of action, rather than try to curtail or control it.

What little is known of these early guilds points to their development predominantly taking place in the more important centres of commercial activity, and Wigan was such a community.

Whatever the facts of the matter – and they are unlikely ever to be known – there is no doubt that by the reign of King John (1199-1216) the power of the merchant guilds was considerable. Over the years they had demonstrated their ability to police their own members, and to use their collective power to generate wealth. They had become respectable, and invariably worked hand-in-hand for the good of the town with the local landowner and civic dignitaries.

The scene was set for the true emergence of the town as a local centre, and for the development of the available local materials and talents.

CHAPTER 2
The Ancient and Loyal Borough

The development of modern Wigan can, rightfully, be said to have started on 26 August 1246 with the granting of several vitally important powers to the town by King Henry III. The wording of the charter is interesting, especially bearing in mind the long-held tradition that the town had already had significant powers royally granted to it over a century earlier. If that had been the case, then the opening paragraph of the royal charter might have been very different. Henry's charter is relatively short, and addressed not to the people of Wigan, but to John Mansel, described as a 'parson' but actually the earliest recorded Rector of Wigan. In it, the King promises that Mansel's lands may be a borough forever!

The charter is here reproduced in full:

> Henry, by the grace of God, King of England, Lord of Ireland, Duke of Normandy, Aquitaine and Count of Angers; to all Archbishops, Bishops, Abbots, Priors, Earls, barons, Justices, Sheriffs, Chief Ministers and Bailiffs, and his faithful subjects, greetings: know ye that we have granted, and by this our charter confirmed for us and our heirs to our beloved and faithful John Mansel, parson of the Church of Wigan, that his lands at Wygayun may be a borough for ever, and that the burgesses of the same borough may have a Guild Merchant, with a treasury and other liberties and free customs to that guild belonging, and that no one who is not of

Along the banks of the River Douglas were the town's first corn mills – probably built in the thirteenth century – and, later, the first cotton mills. The 'old corn mill' at the foot of Coppull Lane was photographed c.1890 by John Cooper. The mill buildings clearly date back to the sixteenth and seventeenth centuries and may have replaced an earlier mill.

that Guild may make any merchandise in the aforesaid borough unless by the will of the same burgesses. We have also granted to the same burgesses and their heirs that they may have rights of local jurisdiction, admission, and attachment within the said borough, and that they may come and go freely, and be free throughout our whole land, and through all the ports of the sea, from toll, custom, passage, pontage, and stallage, and that no Counties or Wapentakes shall have any influence on the tenures which they hold within the borough aforesaid. We have also granted to the same burgesses and their heirs, that whatsoever traders shall come to the borough aforesaid with their merchandise, of whatsoever place they shall be, foreigners, or others, who shall be of our peace, or of our leave, shall come into our land, may come safely and securely to the aforesaid borough with their merchandise, and safely there may stay and safely from thence may return by doing there the right and due customs: we do also prohibit that no one may do injury or damage, or molestation, unto the aforesaid burgesses, upon forfeiture of £10. Wherefore we do will and firmly command for us and our heirs that the aforesaid manor of Wigan be a borough for ever, and that the aforesaid burgesses may have the aforesaid Guild Merchant, with an entry fee and with other liberties and free customs to that Guild belonging, and that they may have all other liberties and free customs and quittances as is aforesaid.

In the early 1970s, the Coat of Arms of the County Borough of Wigan was created in plants in Mesnes Park by the Parks Department gardeners.

Witnesses hereto:- Richard Earl of Cornwall, our brother, Roger le Pygot, Earl of Norfolk, Peter de Saband, William de Ferrers, Ralph Fit Nichol, William de Cantilupo, John de Plesset, Paul Peyner, Robert de Mustengros, Bartholemy Peche and others. Given by our hand at Woodstock, the 26th day of August in the thirtieth year of our reign.

The charter was far reaching in its grants and rights, but despite having created Wigan as a borough – of equal rank with Liverpool, Preston and Lancaster, and considerably outstripping the importance of Manchester – that charter did not herald a unilateral dismantling of the feudal system which had operated for so long. The merchants who became the first burgesses of Wigan were very few, and for the many little changed. For the many, Roger de Mansel was still their master in all matters secular as well as religious.

For the burgesses, however, the charter introduced freedom of action, freedom of movement, and most importantly, freedom of trade. Stallage, for example, gave them the right to set up their stalls in markets throughout the land, free of charge, and sell their wares. Freedom of toll and pontage meant they could travel the turnpike roads and cross bridges without payment.

The power of jurisdiction, however, gave them rights which cut directly across Mansel's traditional powers, as did rights of admission and attachment. To recognise the freedom the King's charter granted to the burgesses, Mansel himself issued a parish charter in the following year, conceding some of his powers to the burgesses, and effectively avoiding a fundamental conflict of interests between the newly created borough and the lord of the manor. Indeed he went further, granting permission to the burgesses to grind 'twenty measures' of corn in his mills each year free of charge, and also guaranteeing that they could take wood from his forests, graze their pigs in those same forests, and graze their sheep and cattle on his pastures in return for a of payment of threepence per quarter!

There would have been a measure of practicality about Mansel's extension of the burgesses' freedom. He was not often in Wigan, having more pressing and profitable obligations further south, and the measure of self-government that he agreed for the town meant that the responsibilities of the burgesses to manage their own affairs within a neatly defined framework freed him from the need always to be there himself.

Mansel was a direct descendent of a Norman baron who had come over with William the Conqueror, and at the time of Wigan's first charter, he

Edward II's Charter, dated 7 June 1314. This was the fourth or fifth Charter granted to the borough.

enjoyed a good relationship with the King, as well as a position of some importance within the church. His manor at Wigan was, therefore, a relatively unimportant part of his estates. According to David Sinclair in his 1882 *History of Wigan*, Mansel was in Germany in 1847, accompanying the Abbot of Westminster Abbey who had been tasked with arranging the future marriage of the daughter of the Duke of Brabant to Prince Edward, the future King Edward I. Whether that story is true or not, Edward actually married Eleanor, daughter of the Duke of Castille, in 1254 as part of a political agreement between the two houses. Again according to Sinclair, Mansel accompanied King Henry III to the enthronement of Boniface as Archbishop of Canterbury in 1249, so his visits to Wigan at the time may have been few and far between.

A second charter from Henry III confirmed and extended the town's autonomous position, but by the time it was issued – April 1258 – Henry's reign was in turmoil.

When the King hit troubled times in the late 1250s after some ill-conceived political decisions, and allegedly failed to heed Mansel's advice, England went through a period of political and military strife, resulting in Henry seeing out the remainder of his life as king in name only. Mansel, apparently, fled to France in 1858. He returned two years later, reconciled with Henry, and briefly held several high offices of state before returning to exile in France once again.

Henry's son, Edward I, had become king in all but name by 1265, eventually acceding to the throne on his father's death in 1272 and reigning until 1307. Despite his preoccupation with troubles with the Scots, he found sufficient time to issue the borough's next charter – in 1292 – which did little more than confirm the promises made by his later father. Indeed, that is a pattern running through several of the charters – confirming rather than extending the rights and privileges enjoyed by the developing town.

But, if stories are to be believed, those privileges were sometimes abused, and sometimes exceeded. Sinclair recounts the story of a court case in 1292, presided over by Adam de Walton, the next known rector after de Mansel, and heard before a jury of burgesses. According to Sinclair's account, a man by the name of Proctor, having been arrested in Wigan, was being tried for the theft of a bull in the Wapentake of Salford. He had, according to the story, been found with the bull in his possession and imprisoned at Wigan Hall!

Proctor was released on bail – against the surety of a merchant by the name of Crowe – to appear before the court on the next day that it sat, some three weeks after his indictment and first appearance. When he failed to appear on the due date, Crowe was allegedly tried for the offence and found guilty by proxy – and hanged!

The tradition of holding a regular open-air market in Wigan may already have been 750 years old by the time this picture was taken in the early years of the twentieth century.

Again according to Sinclair, this event led to the withdrawal of the rights conferred by Henry's charter, the inference being that Edward's charter was issued to reinstate them after pleading on the town's behalf by one John de Bryn, agent of the Banastres. There is no contemporary evidence to support this view – although Sinclair quotes a much later source as confirmation – and the fact that the language used in several later charters mirror's Henry's 1246 wording would seem to suggest that confirming rights granted by their predecessors was a device used by several monarchs to underline their continuing commitment to limited local self-determination.

Whatever the history behind Wigan's thirteenth-century charters, it is assumed that, like elsewhere, they merely conferred legal status on a state of affairs that had been in existence for many years. It is worth noting, with respect to Wigan's claim to have been the recipient of a charter as early as 1100, that Lancaster and Preston have traditionally also believed that their borough status – conferred in 1193 and 1179 respectively – also simply recognised the powers conferred in earlier charters.

Certainly borough status was the spark which lit the flame of commercial development, and the increase in the town's importance as a trading centre. The Guilds Merchant which thrived in boroughs like Wigan were entirely secular – unlike many of the religious or quasi-religious guilds which thrived elsewhere – but they did acknowledge the power of the church, and their activities were dovetailed into the many religious events and fairs which punctuated the calendar. Thus markets and fairs would have been built around religious observances acting as a focal point for the area, bringing many more people into the town – including merchants from elsewhere.

The first chartered market was probably held in the town in 1246 – immediately after Henry III granted borough status – but the tradition may already have been a century old by that time. The likely location of those markets would have been Market Place and that part of Hallgate which we now know as Market Street, and down the slope to the fields

Silcock's Fair was a regular visitor to the Market Square until the 1960s.

where the Galleries Shopping Centre now stands and where, before that, there was the Market Square and the Victorian Market Hall.

The funfair which was held annually on the Market Square until the 1960s, and the Pot Fairs outside the old market hall which remained a feature of Wigan life until the mid-1980s can both trace their roots right back to those early chartered markets and associated events which took place alongside them from the mid-thirteenth century.

Wigan's fourth charter was granted by King Edward II in 1314, and apart from identifying Robert de Clyderhou as Parson of Wigan, does not other than reiterate once again the perpetual powers and privileges granted in 1246. By that time, however, after three quarters of a century of local government, the town was a rather different place.

In 1986, the steel skeleton of the new Market Hall was rising over the old Market Square – the site of open-air markets for well over 800 years. The old market hall can be seen in the distance. It was demolished a little over a year later.

By the end of the thirteenth century, Edward I had introduced a measure of parliamentary representation – known at the Model Parliament – as by recently introduced law, taxes could only be levied with the approval of the people. 'What touches all', the King wrote in the writ, calling that parliament 'should be approved by all, and it is also clear that common dangers should be met by measures agreed upon in common.' With this summons, Edward established the basic principles of English, and later British, democracy.

The parliament was the first at which all Three Estates were all to be represented – Nobility, the Church, and the Commons – and, in 1295, Wigan was one of the relatively few boroughs in England empowered to send two members to that first parliamentary meeting in Westminster.

It is an interesting irony that while today, we celebrate the importance of this action and the importance of Wigan's participation in it, the original parliamentarians found it an irksome inconvenience. It took them away from their lands and their businesses, and they were only too well aware that their journey, for a payment of two shillings per day payable upon their return – with proof that they had participated – was simply to empower the king to tax them! Few people in late thirteenth-century England were aware of the significance of that first convocation at which the commons were represented – although it has to be recognised that the 'commons' were in fact knights, burgesses and those minor landed gentry whose rank placed them just below the nobility but well above the truly common man. The make up of the group of commoners was outlined by the King as:

> We command and firmly enjoin thee that, without delay, thou dost cause to be chosen and to come to us at the time and place aforsaid [at Westminster on the next Sunday after the feast of St. Martin, in winter next coming] two knights of the counties aforesaid; and of every city, two

Scholes Bridge may occupy the approximate site of the first permanent crossing of the River Douglas.

citizens; and of every burgh, two burgesses, of the most discreet and fit for business; so as the said knights may have sufficient power for themselves and the community of the county aforesaid; and the said citizens and burgesses may have the same power, separately for themselves and the cities and burghs, then to do in the premises what shall be ordained by the common council, so that for defect of such power the business aforesaid may not remain undone, and have then the names of the knights, citizens, and burgesses and this writ.

The two burgesses considered to be 'of the most discreet and fit for business' were William Teinterer and Henry le Bocher, but at subsequent parliaments few were willing to take on the onerous duties for a payment which did not cover their costs.

The burgesses representing Wigan at the 1306 parliament were John le Mercer – presumably a textile manufacturer or dealer – and Simon Payer. After that, the town – like many others – apparently ignored its parliamentary duty for over two centuries, believing that the benefits derived from the exercise did not justify the expenses involved.

Thirteenth- and fourteenth-century England had an increasing number of migrant workers, but they were not wholly welcomed by the burgesses of Wigan, keen to maintain their control over employment and wealth generation. While the burgesses were happy to employ the migrants, they were not encouraged to set up home within the borough, instead renting property in the village of Scholes across the river from the town. Luckily for the workers, the first bridge over the Douglas was constructed in the fourteenth century, replacing the ford and stepping stones, and making the crossing a bit less unpleasant for the workers. Given that Millgate was the established route from the town centre to the ford, it is reasonable to assume that the bridge would have crossed the river at about the same point as today's Scholes Bridge near Douglas House. The river being shallow at that point, the bridge would not have needed to be a very substantial affair. For centuries, however, Millgate was subject to frequent flooding at that point, so it may not have offered a dry crossing at all times of the year.

And when those workers came into town in the fourteenth century, they worked at a wide variety of occupations.

Traders would have brought a variety of fuels to the weekly or twice-weekly markets in Wigan. Peat cutting in the boggy lands around the town had been known since before the time of the Romans, and there is evidence that the Romans burned coal in many of their British sites.

Evidence pointing strongly towards coal burning in the first and second centuries was unearthed during the Wiend excavations in the 1980s. So it is not unreasonable to assume that a coal mining industry was already

The huge Alexandra open-cast mining site in Whelley in the late 1980s. Mining in Wigan started with open-cast – but in the fourteenth century, the coal was only just below the surface. Coal extraction at the depth seen here was considered to be deep mining until the nineteenth century, and indeed some eighteenth-century pit workings were uncovered during this open-cast project.

The pewter industry in Wigan was already 400 years old when this eighteenth century tankard was manufactured.

well-established by the beginning of the fourteenth century. The coal seams were, after all, breaking the surface in many places!

The first recorded mention of coal mining in the area comes from a mine in nearby Standish around 1350, but several of the other industries which were already established in the town needed an efficient fuel, and with coal literally lying on the surface, coal would have been an obvious and cheap choice and open-cast mining a logical industrial development.

Miners at the time would have been freemen of the borough – then spelled 'burgh' as it still is in Scotland – but records do not survive which might give us some idea of the scale of the activity.

Several areas of the borough, where the coal lay just below the boggy surface, are recorded as having 'burning wells' where the methane gas seeped up through the standing water and could be ignited by those who knew how to trap it, to the surprise and delights of their audiences!

Pewter manufacture was a part of the Wigan industrial scene for centuries, and required an efficient high temperature fuel to smelt the tin. Originally made of tin and lead, pewter vessels had replaced wooden ones in churches by the beginning of the twelfth century, but presumably only in the highest ranking houses. The Council of Westminster in 1175, however, decreed that pewter vessels should not be used in churches. Perhaps it was a reflection of the increasing power of the church that such a base metal was outlawed, but at a stroke, the pewter-makers had to find new markets for their wares. That market was domestic, and one can easily imagine stalls of simple pewter ware appearing at Wigan's markets throughout the thirteenth and fourteenth centuries. The manufacture of pewter continued in the town well into the eigteenth century.

As the prime source of tin was Cornwall, the smiths or pewterers from Wigan must have made early trading agreements with their suppliers nearly three hundred miles south west. The logistics of getting the material so far north suggests a number of possibilities, perhaps including carriage by sea to Liverpool, or up the Ribble to Tarleton and from there south to Wigan.

Another early industry in Wigan which required a transport infrastructure to be developed and put in place was ceramics. With that one, the raw materials only had to come about fifty miles, but in the fourteenth century even that must have been quite an undertaking.

Of course the other important trade in the town – from at least the thirteenth century – was textiles, and while cotton was a relatively uncommon commodity at that time, wool and flax-based linen textiles were widely worn, and both were certainly spun and woven in the Wigan area.

By the early years of the fourteenth century, records exist of three 'fulling mills' servicing the town's textile industry – two on the River Douglas and one on the Clarington Brook, and the presence of three mills suggests that there must have been quite a number of handloom weavers working in the vicinity.

Fulling mills – where the woven fabrics were washed and degreased – required a constant supply of fuller's earth, a clay-like material which adhered to the natural oils in the fibres, and which could then be washed out. The nearest source of fuller's earth was probably Bala in Wales, requiring the establishment of yet another long and difficult transport route.

Between them – clay from the Midlands, tin from Cornwall, and fuller's earth from Bala – the commodities brought to the town to supply these industries stand testimony to the advanced nature of Wigan's industrial infrastructure, more than six hundred years ago.

It somewhat alters our conceptions of life in the fourteenth and fifteenth centuries when we acknowledge the logistical problems early Wigan manufacturers must have overcome, and the primitive forms of transport at their disposal. With most roads outside of towns no better than rutted tracks, carters could expect to cover only a relatively short distance in a day.

The oldest pottery figure found in Wigan dates from the fifteenth or sixteenth centuries. Pottery, however, is believed to have been manufactured in the town as early as the fourteenth century.

It is remarkable that Wigan was, at the time, engaged in manufacturing industries which produced items of considerable value. A sack of wool for example, cost upwards of £3 and, when spun and woven, even the cheapest woollen fabrics sold for two shillings (10p) per yard. With the average hired labourer on the land or artisan in a manufacturing industry earning no more than £2 to £3 per year in the latter years of the fourteenth century, woollen goods represented a significant outlay. Pottery and pewter ware were probably out of their reach.

The same smelting, alloying and forging skills which were necessary to manufacture pewter also helped develop the town's interests in iron-working, another trade which survived for centuries.

Not all engineering skills would have been focused on metalwork, however – it is likely that woodworking skills were also available locally. The water-powered fulling mills, for example, would probably have been manufactured by local craftsmen. Fulling stocks, the mechanised wooden hammers which pummeled the fabric and fuller's earth together to cleanse the cloth – a practice previously done by treading the material in water – had been introduced before the beginning of the fourteenth century, and it is reasonable to assume they were built locally.

After the Black Death had decimated the workforce in the middle of the fourteenth century – it reached the Wigan area in late 1348 – demand for skilled workmen rose dramatically. Similarly on the land, labour was in short supply, and as a result wages doubled within a year – perhaps the first incidence of wage inflation in Britain! Carried from town to town by the same transportation systems that brought wealth, the disease thrived in the insanitary urban conditions. In that respect Wigan was no different from hundreds of other towns and villages, and learned nothing from the experience. A charter of King Edward III in 1334 had empowered the burgesses to pave the streets of the borough – and build the Douglas Bridge – but a dozen years later those same streets – of what was proudly described as a 'well-paved town' – were little more than an open sewer. The hilly geography of Wigan meant that much of that household waste and effluent flowed down to the River Douglas polluting the water supply on which the residents depended. As a result, and in common with many small towns, Wigan suffered from bad health and low life expectancy – something which would remain an issue for centuries.

However, by the end of the fourteenth century, the town may not have been a pleasant place to live, but it was thriving with a mixed agricultural and industrial economy. The two economies came together in the weekly markets, which were becoming Wigan's shop window.

Apart from the tower of the parish church, only one building survives largely intact from the whole of this early period of Wigan's history – the Boar's Head Inn on the A49 at the border between Wigan and Standish.

The Boar's Head, c.1912. The pub sign announces that George Henry Harmer is a licensed retailer of Foreign and British spirits, and all Porter Wines. Inside, exposed 1,000 year-old beams support the upper floor, and despite Victorian alterations, the pub still retains much of its medieval character.

Originally built as a farmhouse, it has been an inn for centuries. The building can certainly be traced back to the late thirteenth century, and several of the beams in the main bar have been dated at in excess of one thousand years old. Yet, strangely, the building does not even feature in the Lancashire volumes of Nikolaus Pevsner's seminal series *The Buildings of England*.

But for a change of heart forty years ago, the building might not still be standing today. The Ministry of Transport had plans afoot in 1961 to realign the A49, and the inn was in the way. Thankfully for the Boar's Head, the plan was shelved and the pub saved. Unfortunately, the improvements needed to the road in 1961 have never been properly implemented, and the junction, despite the new roundabout, remains a traffic bottleneck.

Di and Malc Meadows ran the Boar's Head Inn until 2008. Successive landlords have endeavoured to maintain the traditional Boar's Head welcome which has kept the pub alive for centuries. The Boar's Head is one of a number of inns which claim to be the second oldest public house in England!

CHAPTER 3
Haigh Hall – History and Legend

Haigh Hall Country Park is one of Wigan's treasures – the huge estates may have been sold off, but the beautiful plantations and the hall itself – one of the ancestral homes of the Earls of Crawford and Balcarres since the eigteenth century – were given to the old County Borough of Wigan for a token price in 1947 to be used for the benefit of the local people. Today it plays host to a number of public events each year, has two fine golf courses, and offers endless walks through beautiful woodland.

Although the present building dates only from the nineteenth century – it was built between 1827 and 1840 – Haigh Hall has played an important role in Wigan's history for centuries. Today's hall is the latest in a succession of great houses to stand on the site. Before work started on the present hall, the building it replaced included traces of a number of architectural styles going back as far as the late thirteenth century – to a period which also saw the building of the oldest parts of Wigan's present parish church.

Estimates of how long the Manor of Haigh and its Lords have played an important role in the life of the area vary from eight to nine hundred years, or even a millennium. The Bradshaighs of Haigh could trace their ancestry back through marriage to the Norreys or Norries, who had held the lands since before the Norman Conquest – although they apparently

Haigh Hall, as seen from the Golf Course. From the hall, Lord Crawford could survey all he controlled. Set on a hill above the town, the terrace offers a magnificent vista over Wigan.

Haigh Hall, in about 1910, as seen from the little canal basin which at the time was used by Wigan Rowing Club (below). The walk along the canal towpath offered fine views of the hall, and was highly popular with the residents of the town. The small dock or basin had originally been constructed for the benefit of the Haigh Foundry, one of the town's most successful early industrial concerns.

lost them after the conquest for a time – so a thousand years is a not unreasonable claim.

The Bradshaigh, or Bradshaghe, family was itself of Saxon origin, with extensive lands in the Blackrod area, and by the time of the marriage of Sir William to Mabel Norreys – sole heiress to the estates of 'Hugh Norres de Haghe and Blackrode' – in the late thirteenth century, it was an established part of the minor nobility, and enjoyed reasonable wealth. Marriage into the Norreys family, with its vast estates, brought a Bradshaigh to Haigh.

If eighteenth and nineteenth century accounts of the architecture of Haigh Hall are to be believed, a house with a chapel attached existed at Haigh before the date of that marriage – usually assumed to be about 1295. Indeed, the thirteenth-century chapel was the sole surviving part of that house by the early nineteenth century.

The Bradshaighs remained at Haigh for almost five centuries, before the estates passed through marriage to the Lindsay family, the Earls of Balcarres and Crawford after whom so many local pubs are still named.

It is worth noting that many of the earliest families to be mentioned in connection with Wigan, all exercised influence for centuries – long after the upheavals of the Norman Conquest were consigned to history. Thus the Standish family, the Gerards, the Woodcocks, the de Hollands, the Bankes and the Bradshaighs figure in the shaping of the fortunes of Wigan and its environs right up until the nineteenth century. In addition to controlling vast tracts of local lends, they became the coal barons, and industrial magnates of the Industrial Revolution and beyond.

To every Wiganer, one story is forever connected with Haigh Hall and with the Bradshaighs – the Legend of Mab's Cross. And just about every Wiganer believes it to be true – although in fact the real story of Lady Mabel Bradshaigh's plight is very different from the legend.

The Victorian romantic novelist Sir Walter Scott first heard the story in the very early 1800s when, visiting the old Haigh Hall as a guest, he was told about Lady Mabel over an after-dinner smoke with Lord Crawford. Scott saw the romantic potential of the story, and decided to explore it as an idea for a novel. In the course of his research, however, he found that the story was not exclusive to Wigan, or even to England. There was at least one version of the story set at Neidpath Castle in Scotland, and yet another set in a German castle overlooking the River Rhine.

Fascinated by the story, however, Scott initially wove it briefly into his 1814 novel *Waverley*. Later, in his 1825 *Tales of the Crusaders*, which also contained the novelette *The Talisman*, the story featured heavily in the sub-plot of *The Betrothed*.

It is a fascinating feature of so many folk legends, that even when the truth is widely available, it is the legend which endures – and so it is with the story of Lady Mabel. The romance of the legend – even although it is

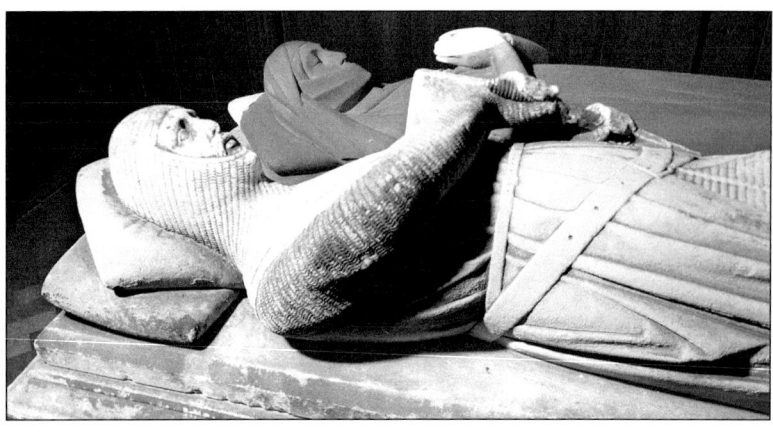

The effigies of Sir William and Lady Mabel Bradshaigh, lie together on their tomb in Wigan Parish Church.

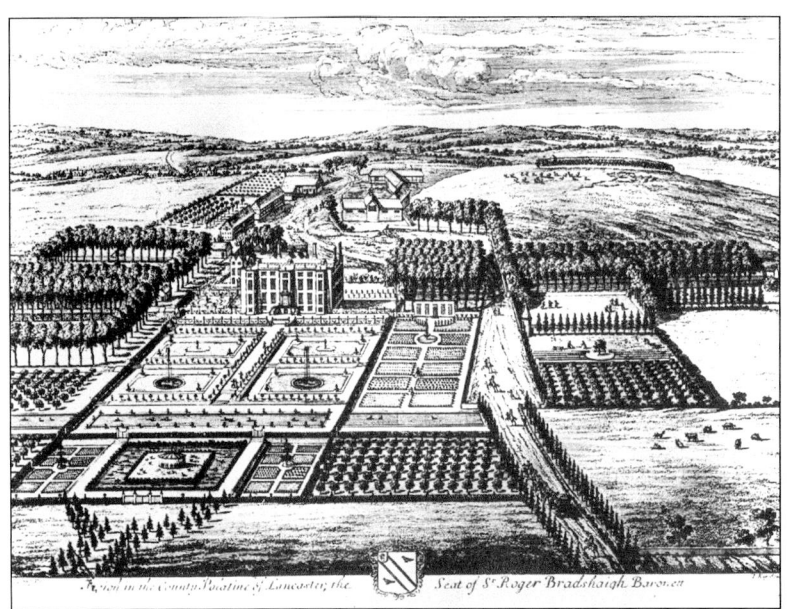

This view of Haigh Hall, from an eighteenth-century engraving, shows the house and garden before the site was cleared in the nineteenth century and the present hall erected.

shared with several other locations – is still preferred to the truth, which perhaps paints Sir William in a less heroic light.

In the introduction to *The Betrothed* Scott acknowledges the source of the idea for the story – and his visit to Haigh Hall – and quotes from the Bradshaigh family version of the legend.

According to the Bradshaighs,

> of this Mabel is a story by tradition of undoubted verity that in Sr William Bradshaghe's absence (beinge 10 yeares away in the wares) she married a Welsh kt. Sir William retorninge from the wares came in a Palmers habit amongst the poore to haghe. Who when she saw and congetringe that he favoured her former husband wept, for which the kt chasticed her at wich Sr William went and made him selfe knawne to his Tenants in wch space the kt fled. But neare to Newton Parke Sr William over-tooke him and slue him. The said Dame Mabell was enoiyned by her confessor to doe Pennances by going onest every week barefoot and bare legg'd to a Crosse ner Wigan from the haghe wilest she lived and is called Mabb X to this day; and ther monument lyes in wigan Church as you see ther portrd.

The most popular version of the legend claims that 'the wares' at which Sir William was away fighting were the Crusades, while another version has him fighting the Scots in the armies of King Edward II. Both versions justify Lady Mabel's actions – after her husband's long absence and the reasonable assumption that he has dead – and there is no doubt that, for a widowed heiress without a husband, a second marriage would have been expected.

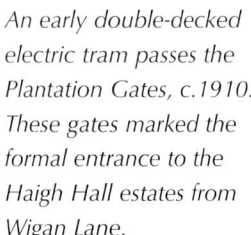

An early double-decked electric tram passes the Plantation Gates, c.1910. These gates marked the formal entrance to the Haigh Hall estates from Wigan Lane.

The story has a number of inconsistencies, which point to it being a later invention. Mabel is recorded as having had a child by Sir William in 'the eighth year of the reign of Edward II – which was 1315, an unlikely twenty years after the date often given for their marriage. There is no further record of this child, and on her death in 1348, Lady Mabel – who had been genuinely widowed since Sir William was slain in a fight in 1333 – bequeathed the Haigh estates to Sir William's nephew, William de Bradshaghe, suggesting that Sir William had had no direct descendant.

Lady Mabel was an undoubtedly religious woman and founded chantry chapels in the two churches most directly associated with her families – Blackrod and Wigan. Of the Blackrod Chantry no trace remains, but the chapel built on to Wigan parish church, modified and rebuilt several times in the intervening 650 years still remains, now known as the Lindsay Aisle.

The Mab's Cross story is traditionally given credence by a carving on the side of their tomb which shows Lady Mabel doing penance before a cross with an uncanny resemblance to that which now bears her name.

The true story is rather less romantic, rather more violent and in keeping with the times, and depicts Sir William as rather less of a hero. The seventh and final Crusade had been over for several years before Sir William's marriage to Lady Mabel, so it is easy to dismiss that version. Wars with Scotland were certainly ongoing – at the time of his marriage the English armies were fighting William Wallace, and by 1314 they were suffering their most ignominious defeat at the Battle of Bannockburn. So, if Sir William had been away 'at the wares', it would most probably have been in Scotland. Whether or not he was, however, the true story of Lady Mabel's misery comes, in fact, from the aftermath of that huge military defeat by the Scots.

In many respects Edward II was an incompetent king, and one who was unwilling to take advice. The defeat of his armies at Bannockburn – under his personal leadership and using his own strategy – was a major humiliation for him, and led directly to a dispute with his barons over, amongst other things, the use (or abuse) of both royal and baronial power. The ensuing squabble was not about right or wrong, but about who wielded the most power, the king or his barons. Edward had, on occasions, tried to buy allegiance by rewarding supporters with tracts of land which were rightly the property of others, and dissent amongst the barons – even those who shared his military and political aims – came to a head in October 1315.

With little credibility left after his defeat, Edward was more dependent upon the support of the barons than he wished to be – seeing that dependency as a threat to what personal authority he had left – while the barons saw this as an opportunity to extract concessions and guarantees from the king. Foremost in this movement was the Duke of Lancaster, whose stated was said to have been a wish to restore stability and good governance in England. Sadly, he too was weak and incompetent, and a group of knights stood out in opposition to his plans, seeing his methods as a weakening of their limited power and authority. Amongst them were Sir Adam Banastre, Sir William Bradshaigh and a number of other local knights. Banastre was their leader, and under his headship, they harried their opponents – including the de Hollands of Holland Hall. Bradshaigh and the other rebels were effectively 'wanted men', and a sworn indictment of Bradshaigh at the time declared that 'Sir William Bradshaghe is a common evildoer' and that he should be hunted down. He fled the area, while Lancaster's men hunted down his co-conspirators and killed them. By 1319, when there was a law suit over the ownership of one of the Bradshaigh estates at Anderton near Blackrod, he was actually declared to be dead.

After Lancaster – the King's cousin – was arrested and beheaded at Pontefract Castle in 1322, Bradshaigh returned to Wigan, but was himself arrested and imprisoned two years later.

He was eventually released, and lived out the remainder of his life at Haigh – losing his life in 1333 at Newton, slain by a kinsman of one of the knights he had attacked in 1315 soon after joining Banastre on the rampage.

There is no place in this much harsher story for a bigamous marriage, a slain Welsh knight at Newton, or a barefoot weekly pilgrimage to Wigan Cross – and yet the sculpture of Lady Mabel on her knees at the foot of the cross was included in the decoration of one side of her tomb. Perhaps the sculptor who created the relief panel simply wished to show her at her devotions, or perhaps praying for the safe return of Sir William from exile.

A hundred years ago Mab's Cross was protected behind cast-iron railings outside the fine Georgian town house at the top of Standishgate which is now known as the Mab's Cross Hotel. It was moved to the opposite side during road alterations in 1921, and now sits outside Mab's Cross Primary School.

Or perhaps the relief tableaux on the tomb, like the legend, were a later attempt by the family to draw a veil across this whole sorry episode. The fiction is, by far, more alluring than the facts. Certainly the tomb cannot be dated, and may therefore have been created many years later. The legend of Mab's Cross itself does not appear in any of the family records until 1647.

Another tableau on the tomb is said to depict the slaying of the Welsh knight by Sir William, but it could just as easily be read as the image of his own death. By a roadside in Newton-le-Willows is a strangely shaped red stone, known locally as the 'Bloody Stone', and just as Mab's Cross marks the site of lady Mabel's legendary penance, the Bloody Stone marks the site of Sir William's legendary slaying of the Welsh knight. But could it, perhaps, mark the spot of his own death?

We can assume that Lady Mabel's child, born 1315, either did not outlive Sir William, or was a daughter – the laws of entailment ensured succession by the eldest son or the closest male heir. That would explain Lady Mabel passing the estates to her nephew William de Bradshaghe on her death in 1348. While the succession from that nephew is chronicled, there are apparently no recorded events of local or national significance linked to the family.

By the middle of the fifteenth century the Bradshaighs had links by marriage with the Standish family, and over the ensuing century, the family's power and influence increased considerably.

In 1535 Sir Roger Bradshaigh was amongst a group of Lancashire knights who earned the thanks of Henry VIII for their part in suppressing an uprising against the King, but until the outbreak of the Civil War, the family lived a relatively quiet existence in their Wigan estate.

Although usually referred to as Bradshaigh today, some sources assert that the family retained the Bradshaghe spelling until the early years of the sixteenth century, but as written language was a variable thing at the time, both spellings of the name can be found up until the Civil War years.

Successive generations of the family continued to be interred in the private chapel in Wigan parish church long after the Reformation, and their remains were still there when the family vault was last opened, about fifty years ago.

Haigh Hall itself underwent several rebuildings throughout the family's long period of occupation, reflecting the building styles of each period – a necessary public demonstration of wealth and status. It has, at times, been a timbered mansion, a fine Jacobean house, and now a Victorian one.

But long before the present mansion was built, the last of the male Bradshaigh heirs had died, and the last Bradshaigh to control estates was a woman – Dame Dorothy. After her death in 1785, the estates passed to Elizabeth Bradshaigh Dalrymple, by that time the wife of Alexander Lindsay, 6th Earl of Balcarres. He visited Haigh from time to time to keep an eye on the family's mining and industrial interests – which were in a rather rundown condition when he and his wife inherited – but his main homes were in Edinburgh and London until 1802, when on his retirement from the post of Governor of Jamaica, he settled in Wigan. By 1808 he had also inherited the title of 23rd Earl of Crawford, the two titles being used jointly thereafter. By the time of his death in 1825, the family fortunes were in the ascendancy, with increasing demand for coal and iron, and his son James further developed the family's industrial interests.

The wealth accrued through coal and iron – they controlled the powerful Wigan Coal and Iron Company – allowed the family to live in luxury, and enabled successive earls to develop the estates, build up an important library of antiquarian and historical books – now in Manchester's John Ryland Library – and purchase a luxurious yacht. They are also remembered for endowing almshouses for retired estate workers, and other charitable undertakings.

In the nineteenth and twentieth centuries, the family produced a number of eminent academics, military leaders, and artists. Their interests embraced a wide range of British cultural organisations – especially associated with museums and art galleries.

Successive members of the family over the years served in parliament, some in the Commons, many in the Lords – and a number even styled themselves as Baron of Wigan.

The Lindsays held the estates for a 160 years before their generous gift to the County Borough in 1947. The 28th Earl, who could trace his ancestry back to Hugh Norreys in 1193, the last resident owner of Haigh, sold the estates and moved the family seat back to Balcarres in Fife.

Walking up the drive from the Plantation Gates to Haigh Hall was both popular and permitted in the early years of the twentieth century, despite the estates still being very much in private hands.

CHAPTER 4
Tudor and Elizabethan Wigan and Beyond

The fifteenth century is mostly remembered in the north of England for the Wars of the Roses, between the Lancastrians and Yorkists. The war had come about over the succession – Henry VI was at the time childless, and his wife, Queen Margaret, widely hated.

Then, Edward, Prince of Wales was born in 1453 and legally, the succession should have been secure. The King's ill-health, however, gave the Queen immense power, and she determined to crush the house of York, the main rivals to the throne. After six years of war, Henry was deposed, and the eighteen-year-old Edward of York was elected to the throne. Eventually, after a further ten years of revolt and skirmish, the Lancastrians reluctantly accepted the rule of the new king – Edward IV – but, while the turmoil seems only to have lightly touched the people of Wigan, elsewhere mayhem continued. Edward IV died at the age of 40, and his twelve-year-old son, Edward V reigned for only three months before apparently being murdered in the Tower of London. The remains of a twelve-year old-boy of similar stature to the boy-King were discovered in the Tower as recently as 1933. The trouble continued throughout the

In the late nineteenth century this sixteenth-century inn was known as the Queen's Head. It was demolished in the 1890s.

Across the river in Scholes, remnants of the medieval town could also still be found in the 1880s. The building housing this butcher's shop, squeezed in between later buildings, clearly dates back to the fifteenth or sixteenth century.

reign of Richard III, and was briefly resolved when the houses of York and Lancaster were united in marriage in 1486 when Henry Tudor married Elizabeth of Lancaster, however, the birth of their first son caused the Lancastrians to revolt again. Their rivalry continued to flare up until the end of the fifteenth century.

As far as Wigan is concerned, little is known of this period in history. The war was probably seen as a diversion from the primary pursuit of commerce. The freedoms enjoyed by the burgesses, protected by their guild, excused them from any call to arms, although men further down the social ladder were not so lucky.

The people of Wigan were, generally speaking, followers of Henry of Richmond, although most of those pressed to take up arms probably knew little of the opposing views, and merely followed the bidding of their masters. According to Sinclair in his 1882 *History of Wigan* the town's archers practised each day in preparation for the coming battle on the meadow in front of Wigan school, then down by the Douglas.

The only mention of Wigan during the struggle comes from a rhyme about the Battle of Bosworth – which was fought on August 22, 1485 – which relates the capture of Richard III's banner by Lord Stanley's army.

> *Jack of Wigan, he did take*
> *The Duke of Gloucester's banner,*
> *And hung it up in Wigan Church,*
> *A monument of honour*

A contemporary portrait of Thomas Linacre, 1460-1524, founder of the College of Physicians in 1518, and Rector of Wigan between 1519 and 1524.

Just who 'Jack of Wigan' was, history does not confirm, although he may well have been Sir James Bradshaigh, who would have been in his early forties at the time. It would not unreasonable to assume that the suffix *of Wigan* might usually have been applied to the lord of the manor.

On Bosworth field, Richard was defeated and killed, Henry Tudor was crowned King Henry VII, and Stanley was granted the title of the first Lord Derby.

In the early years of the sixteenth century, and at the end of a long and distinguished career, Thomas Linacre was appointed Rector of Wigan. Linacre was a physician of some renown as well as a cleric, and for a time was the personal physician to Henry VII, and later to Henry VIII. He was also personal physician to Cardinal Wolsey, Archbishop Warham, and Bishop Fox, and his close association with the clergy may have been instrumental in him seeking entry to the priesthood late in life. He had held several clerical positions for many years, despite not being a priest himself at the time, but with his public life behind him, he determined to take Holy Orders. He was ordained as a priest in 1520, at the age of sixty – although his appointment to Wigan was confirmed on 19 October in the previous year – and Wigan may have been his first and only clerical appointment, for he died four years later at the age of sixty-four.

Linacre was also a classical scholar – having studied Greek in Florence with the sons of Lorenzo de Medici (one of whom went on to become Pope Leo X) under the great scholar Angelo Poliziano – and was one of a group of intellectuals surrounding both Henry VII and Henry VIII who brought about considerable changes in English academia.

Since graduating at the age of twenty-four he had been a Fellow of All Souls College in Cambridge. He then travelled extensively, and studied abroad for several years, gaining his medical qualifications in Padua. He

Wigan Grammar School founded before the reign of Queen Elizabeth I, moved to a site on Parsons Walk in 1936. Its 1950s extension – now part of Wigan and Leigh College – included the Linacre Theatre. Today the refurbished 1936 buildings house the Thomas Linacre Centre – Wigan Infirmary's Outpatients Department.

The John Bull Chop House in Cooper's Row behind Market Place is typical of the type of buildings in Wigan in the seventeenth and eighteenth centuries.

is best known in Britain, however, for founding the College of Physicians in 1518 – the oldest medical organisation in England and now the Royal College of Physicians. The first home of the College, formed by a charter of Henry VIII, was Linacre's London house. It is fitting, therefore, that the new Outpatients Department of Wigan's Royal Infirmary, in the former Wigan Grammar School building, should have been named the Thomas Linacre Centre, linking the great doctor's name with medicine in the town.

As he died in 1524 – becoming the only Rector of Wigan to be buried in St Paul's Cathedral in London – Linacre was spared any of the anguish which came with Henry's disputes with Rome which brought about the English Reformation. Wigan itself was barely touched by it – being a town built around industry rather than a religious community. Indeed, although the Act of Dissolution was passed in 1536, and the monastic system had been almost completely dismantled by 1540, the Catholic Mass was still being celebrated in Wigan parish church until at least 1548, the year in which an Act of Parliament closed all chantries and chantry chapels – including the Bradshaigh chantries at Wigan and Blackrod.

In 1514, Henry VIII had issued a charter which protected the rights of foreign traders to sell their wares at borough markets throughout England, and at the same time, introduced a 'minimum wage' of fivepence halfpenny a week for skilled employees, thus effectively making foreign goods more expensive than locally produced ones!

The situation for local master craftsmen seems to have steadily deteriorated until in 1534 it is recorded that a number of them rebelled, destroying the stalls of foreign traders at Wigan Fair, and resulting in quite the opposite effect to that which they had intended – for they were all arrested, tried at Lancaster Assizes and found guilty!

The seventeenth-century seal of the town included this representation of the Town Hall built in the reign of Henry VIII. The building itself was demolished in the eighteenth century.

The 'pavid' streets of Wigan in the sixteenth century would have looked very like this ancient cobbled stretch of Cooper's Row with its flagged cart tracks.

Two silver sixpences from the reign of Queen Elizabeth. The date on the upper coin – the size of today's 10p – is indecipherable, but the other is clearly dated 1561.

A few years later, in 1540, the diarist John Leland wrote that,

> Wigan, pavid as bigge as Warringtoun, and better builded; there is one Paroch Church amidde the Towne, summe Marchuantes, sum Artificers, sum fermers. Mr Bradshaghe has a place caullid Haghe, a mile from Wigan; He has found moch Canal like Se Coole in his ground very profitable to him and Gerade, of Ynse, dwellith in that parish. The great Myne, of Canale, is at haghe, 2 miles from Wigan. One Bradshaghe dwellith at Haghe.

Clearly mining of cannel, or candle, coal was already a well-established industry. It was so named because of the brightness of the flame with which it burned. In later years, it would be carved and polished to create anything from sculptures to dinner plates, and a story endures of a nineteenth-century dinner party at Haigh being served on cannel plates, which were then cast into the open fire.

A summer house was constructed entirely of cannel in the grounds of Haigh Hall in the seventh century, and was reportedly still standing when Sir Walter Scott visited Lord Crawford in the early years of the nineteenth century!

The religious upheavals which followed Henry VIII's split with Rome in the 1530s brought turmoil to Wigan and its environs – and turmoil which lasted through to the end of Elizabeth's reign almost seventy years later. Both sides had their martyrs in the second half of the century as, first, Bloody Mary sought to crush Protestantism and reimpose the rule of the Catholic Church after she succeeded Henry to the throne and, later, as Elizabeth's initial attempt at religious tolerance turned into the strongly anti-Catholic policies for which she is better remembered. Given the number of families in the area who clung on to the Catholic faith long after it was outlawed, it is not surprising that the area felt the growing religious oppression fiercely.

Many of the great families of the areas surrounding the town were less willing to adopt the new religious order than the townsfolk, so while the transition from the Roman church to the Anglican church in the town seems to have been a relatively low key affair, in the surrounding estates and villages, it was anything but!

By the middle of Henry VIII's reign, Wigan, as a parliamentary borough had, like many others, failed to take its parliamentary duties seriously – cost and apathy meaning that for close on two hundred years no representatives had been sent to Westminster. A change of heart, or improved financial support, reversed that trait, and the names of several of the town's representatives are recorded. From 1547 until 1552, Thomas Carus and Thomas Barlow were returned for the borough – but neither was a local Wigan man. Barlow was a Mancunian, and Carus came from Kirby

Lonsdale and later sat for Lancaster. Barlow continued to serve the borough until 1557. Successive MPs were from outside the town. In 1558, William Gerard and Thomas Bromley sat for the town, Gerard came from Preston and Bromley was a renowned London barrister. He went on to become Lord Keeper of the Great Seal under Elizabeth I.

For the sons of the wealthy, Wigan Grammar School had been established by 1596 – but it was not the first school in the town. Earlier accounts of archers practicing on the school common point to a school having been in existence as early as the reign of Richard III.

As the sixteenth century drew to a close, Wigan was still a relatively small town – population estimates vary from 4,000 to 5,000 – and probably about the same size as Manchester!

But by that time, the seeds of the great industries of the eigteenth and nineteenth centuries were beginning to sprout. Cotton was a developing industry – while wool and flax were in decline – and demand for coal was also growing.

On the religious front, Puritanism had come to Wigan, initially amongst the cotton spinners and weavers. The Puritan movement initially began as a protect again Elizabeth I's attempts early in her reign to find a middle ground which embraced religious tolerance. By the time the Queen changed her position, the Puritan movement was more concerned with establishing 'purer' Protestant principles within the Church of England. It has been surmised that Puritanism came to Wigan as a result of powerful cotton merchants in London who chose to buy product only from those who shared their religious beliefs. When the Puritan movement became increasingly political, tension between it and the crown increased dramatically, and eventually led to civil war.

Traces of the sixteenth-century town survived into the twentieth century. This ancient building, close to the junction of Millgate and Chapel Lane, was photographed c.1900.

CHAPTER 5
Wigan During the Civil War

The seventeenth century might have been expected to bring with it much needed peace – the Union of the Crowns bringing together the nations of England and Scotland under Scotland's King James VI, re-styled as James I. James had become King of Scotland as an infant, after his mother, Mary Queen of Scots, had been deposed in 1567. She was executed twenty years later on the orders of her cousin, Elizabeth I and, on Elizabeth's death in 1603 at the age of sixty-nine, he was the closest heir.

But religious and political discontent were still rife throughout England, and less than two years into his reign, the Catholic-inspired Gunpowder Plot was hatched, leading to further violent repression of Catholics. At the other end of the religious spectrum, the King came under severe criticism by the Puritans, who believed that the Church of England was still too much like the Church of Rome – amongst other things, they eschewed vestments, and any other trappings of religious observance which were not expressively sanctioned by the New Testament.

The population of Wigan was still divided along Protestant and Catholic lines throughout the reign of James I and into the reign of Charles I who acceded to the throne in 1625. Sometimes even families were split because of this religious divide. The gulf between the monarch and his parliament was growing ever wider as a result of parliament's authority in all matters relating to tax-raising being usurped by the King, and tension within the Church of England was growing ever greater as Puritanism gained greater popularity.

When the Puritans began to feel that they were being squeezed out of the Church of England, they sought political allies amongst the parliamentary opposition who shared their concerns both over the King's growing disregard for Parliament, and his policies of leniency towards Catholics.

Amongst those who felt that religious purity could only be achieved with a completely fresh start, a small band under the military leadership of Myles Standish sought permission to settle in America, and set sail on the *Mayflower* in 1620. Contrary to widely held beliefs in Wigan, Myles Standish was not from Standish Hall – which used to stand on the Wigan-Standish border – but had been born in the Isle of Man, into a minor branch of the family. As a result, there is now a town called Standish in the New World, and, although its whereabouts is unknown, the timbered

Great Hall of Standish Hall is believed to have been sold to an American by the French widow of Henry Standish in 1921. The Pilgrims found their religious freedom on the east coast of America, but for those who stayed at home, decades of turmoil lay ahead.

The sort of polarisation of opinion, both political and religious, which typified the early years of the seventeenth century was always going to tear Wigan apart – as the religious makeup of the community had necessitated a degree of tolerance. In 1627, for example, the two Royalist members returned to King Charles's third parliament reflected this tolerance – Sir Anthony St John, who had represented Wigan since 1623, was a Catholic, while Edward Bridgeman was a Protestant. Five other candidates stood for election, including two other avowed Royalists, and three local craftsmen who, not being burgesses of the town, were strictly speaking, ineligible. Those days were, of course, still a long way from universal franchise, and St John actually beat Bridgeman into second place by only two votes – polling 65 and 63 votes respectively. For the majority of Wiganers, barred from voting, such elections were of no interest whatsoever. In 1627 the electoral role contained a mere 138 names. Of those, only 74 chose to vote, and four of them voted only for a single candidate. Four of the candidates only gained one vote each, and the fifth only eight! By 1639 there were 296 burgesses, listed as either out-burgesses or in-burgesses – identifying them as living within the town itself or in the surrounding estates. Amongst those who successfully stood for election was Orlando Bridgeman, who polled eight more votes than his nearest rival and was due elected to the 1640 Parliament.

Standish Hall as it looked at the end of the sixteenth century. The timbered Great Hall was later flanked by Georgian additions, until it was dismantled in 1921 and sold, apparently to an American, although all trace of it has disappeared. The Georgian wing to the left of the hall survived into the early 1980s, having been used for a time as a pigsty! Then it too was demolished.

Sir Orlando Bridgeman, elected MP for Wigan in 1639, served from 1640, and was expelled from the House on 29 April 1642. He was the son of the onetime Rector of Wigan, John Bridgeman, later Bishop of Chester, and himself became Lord Keeper of the Great Seal in the early 1660s at the court of King Charles II.

That Parliament had been heralded as a possible instrument for change, and there was, apparently, wider than usual interest in it. Sinclair, in his 1882 *History of Wigan* wrote that:

> When the names of all the registered voters was called over, a new but not unexpected incident took place. There had been many fiery electioneering speeches made during the preceding week. The were well-to-do people in the town, who were treated equally with burgesses, but who had not taken the burgess oath, and been formally enrolled in the book kept for the purpose. They declared they were entitled to vote, and in violent speeches publicly mentioned they were to vote, and if they were not allowed they were determined to petition Parliament against the election, and so unseat the members and have a new election.

The election was over, but not the excitement, for the intense interest which the 'handicraftsmen and inferior persons' had taken in the exercise of the franchise had fixed in them that unreasonable conviction that there could be no fair election in which they were not privileged to take a part. It was impossible to prove their claims were illegal, but it was just as impossible to prove that they were legal, and therefore those in authority disallowed their claims.

An interesting legal anomaly had come to light. While the first charter in 1246 had obliged two burgesses to be elected and sent to take part in Parliament, no mention had been made of how they should be elected, or by whom. It was clear that the members of parliament had to be burgesses, but nowhere did it say that only burgesses could elect them – yet that had been the case at every election for 400 years! So what constituted a burgess? Today we recognise that a burgess is a resident of a burgh who had acquired full municipal powers and rights – but it is highly probable that in mediaeval England those rights were granted by those already enjoying them, making the role of burgesses rather a closed and exclusive group.

The Bridgeman family name is remembered in the elegant street of Victorian Town Houses which overlooks the Mesnes Park – Bridgeman Terrace, seen here in an early postcard c.1910.

The other member returned for Wigan in 1639 was Alexander Rigby, and the election of the two men encapsulated the dichotomy that faced the town – Bridgeman was staunchly Protestant and Royalist, while Rigby, a devout Puritan, was a supporter of the Parliamentary cause. They took their places in what became known as the 'Short Parliament', which in fact met for only three weeks before the King dissolved it on 5 May 1640. A new election was called, resulting in what became known as the 'Long Parliament', but as if to emphasise how rapidly the political tide was turning, both men were re-elected, but this time Rigby polled the highest number of votes – 136 to 128.

The days of universal suffrage were, as has already been mentioned, still centuries in the future – and so were the days of secret ballot. The election was held in the Town Hall, and as each burgess's name was read out from a roll, he declared his vote. In that 1640 election, there were 123 burgesses and a further 173 'honorary burgesses' who had taken the oath and paid the 'fine' to register themselves on the electoral role. All but fourteen of the burgesses turned up but, surprisingly, of those who had bought their right to vote, fewer than one third exercised the rights they had purchased!

Everything changed in April 1642, however, when the Royalist Bridgeman was expelled from Westminster by the Parliamentarians – his loyalty to the King was seen as disloyalty to Parliament – and until the election of John Holcroft in March 1646, Wigan's representation was down to one.

Long before that, however, the two sides were on a collision course, and the whole picture had been further complicated a few years earlier in 1639 by an uprising in Scotland. The King had fled from London in January 1642, and would not return again until December 1648, a few weeks before his execution.

Locally, families were split by conflicting loyalties, and adjacent towns which had previously worked and prospered together found themselves in opposition – Wigan, for example, was predominantly Royalist, while Bolton's colours were firmly allied to the Parliamentarians.

War broke out in earnest in August 1642 when the king rallied supporters around his royal standard at Nottingham, and in the following month, the first skirmish of the war in the north-west of England took place at Manchester with a small Royalist force led by Lord Strange – who only a few weeks into the campaign inherited the title of Lord Derby. By November 1642, Derby's forces were briefly encamped just outside Wigan, and Derby himself was headquartered in the town. His forces became known for a time as the 'Wigan Cavaliers', and after spending some months further south, they were back in Lancashire in early 1643, attempting – and failing – to take Bolton, but successfully capturing

A Cavalier spur found near Wigan.

Preston. After that a substantial proportion of the force was withdrawn to Lathom House near Ormskirk, to protect the home of Lord Derby, and the inevitable happened – Wigan fell to the Roundheads. It was during this encounter that a group of Royalists barricaded themselves in the tower of Wigan parish church, agreeing to come out only when the Parliamentarian Colonel Rosworm threatened to blow it up with them still inside. Eighty-six men had held out in the tower, but as they gave themselves up, the Parliamentary forces rode off, apparently leaving Rosworm and a few soldiers surrounded by irate Wiganers. He is reported to have mounted his horse and fled!

The Roundhead forces were back three weeks later, however, this time finding no resistance whatsoever, and by 22 April, Wigan was once more in Parliamentary hands.

Lord Derby's wife wrote to the King's cousin, prince Rupert, after the April attack on Wigan, entreating him to come to the town's aid, but he

It was in the ancient tower of All Saints Parish Church that eighty-six Cavaliers took refuge during the first siege of the town on 1 April 1643. They eventually gave themselves up when the Roundheads threatened to blow it up.

was far south an unable to offer immediate assistance. She wrote from Lathom House:

> My Lord,
> I have just received the disastrous news of the loss of Wigan, six miles from this place. It has held out for only two hours having been panic-struck. My husband was twelve miles off and before he was ready to succour it, it was surrendered. In the name of god, my Lord, take pity on us; and if you appear you can conquer it easily, and with much honour to Your Highness. Have pity on my husband, my children, and me who are lost forever if God and your Highness do not take pity on us.

By the time the letter reached Prince Rupert, the town was probably back in Royalist hands – or may indeed have fallen for the second time. A letter from the King to the Mayor of Wigan on 25 February 1644 recognised the town's loyalty:

> Trusty and Wellbeloved, Wee Greet you well. Whereas We have received particular information of the singular affection you have lately expressed in your great expense, approved fidelity, and indefatigable industry against the rebels in those parts, We doe hereby return Our Royal Thanks for the same, and assure you We will always remember your loyal and faithful endeavours in Our service abovsayd upon all occasions for your advantage, And soe We bid you heartily farewell. Given att Our Court att oxford, the 25th of February in the eighteenth year of our reign.

The date of that letter is interesting, for in February 1644, the town was still in Roundhead hands. Indeed, Prince Rupert's attempts to capture it back did not materialise until May 1644. He succeeded, with cavalry units headed by Lord Derby, and reportedly the Roundhead garrison at Bolton was slaughtered to a man on 28 May.

The Royalist successes were short-lived, however, and after the Battle of Marston Moor, Wigan was eventually recaptured by the Roundheads, and Lathom House was sacked and razed to the ground.

Two military helmets from the Civil Wars – now part of the Wigan Heritage and Cultural Trust Collection.

The first Civil War was all but over when the Royalists suffered that major defeat at Marston Moor on 2 July 1644 and in the following year Cromwell instigated the New Model Parliament. The King, who had sought refuge with the Scots was surrendered to the Parliamentarians in the following year, 1646, but escaped to the Isle of Wight where he was kept virtually under house arrest. Until 1648 the town enjoyed a period of relative peace.

In 1848, the Royalist cause was strengthened by the Scottish Duke of Hamilton raising an army and moving south. When they were confronted by Cromwell's forces near Preston, a three-day battle ensued, with the fighting moving steadily south towards Standish. At one point Hamilton's infantry entered Wigan, pillaging as they went, and Cromwell's account of the battle from a Roundhead point of view tells it all:

> At last the enemy [the Scots] drew up within three miles of Wigan; and by the time our army was come up, they drew off again and recovered Wigan before we could attempt anything upon them. We lay that night in a field close by the enemy; being very dirty and weary, and having marched twelve miles of such ground as I never rode in my life, the day being very wet [the roads were apparently virtually impassable after a spell of prolonged torrential rain]. We had some skirmishing that night with the enemy near the town; where we took General van Druske and a colonel, and killed some principal officers, and took a hundred prisoners; where I also received a letter from the Duke of Hamilton, for a civil usage towards his kinsman Colonel Hamilton who had been wounded there . . .

And of the pillaging that night by the members of Hamilton's defeated infantry, Cromwell wrote 'the townspeople of Wigan, a great and poor town, and very malignant [i.e. Royalist] were plundered to their skins by them.'

Cromwell's victory was complete, and to drive home the point, John Holcroft, who had replaced Orlando Bridgeman as one of the members of parliament for Wigan, found himself barred from the house – like so many other Royalist sympathisers – leaving a house filled with members entirely supportive of Cromwell. This became known as the 'Rump Parliament', and on 28 December 1648 voted to send the King for trial on charges asserting that he was a 'tyrant, traitor, murderer, public and implacable enemy of the commonwealth of England.'

On 30 January 1649, the King was executed and the Commonwealth was declared, led by Cromwell – but not yet as Lord Protector, a title he assumed in 1653. In Scotland, however, Charles II was declared King, so clearly the war was far from over.

It was with King Charles II at its head that a second army of Scots moved south into Lancashire in summer 1651, and by mid-August the Scottish troops were in Wigan.

The town which the army found was very different to the staunchly Royalist borough of the first Civil War. The Rector of Wigan, James Bradshawe – appointed in 1645 because the previous incumbent was not strict enough – had been ejected in 1650 for his failure to observe all the requirements laid down by parliament. His replacement in was a Puritan, Charles Hotham, and persecution of local Catholics was widespread. Hotham, the only Puritan ever to hold the title of Rector of Wigan,

A highly decorated Cavalier breastplate (top) and a plainer one (above) from the Civil Wars – now part of the Wigan Heritage and Cultural Trust Collection.

The wooded slopes of the Douglas valley, between Wigan Lane and the river, were the scene of the pivotal Battle of Wigan Lane on 25 August 1651.

remained in office until well after the fall of the Commonwealth.

Lord Derby, at that time in exile in the Isle of Man, quickly set sail with his forces to meet with the King's, and the two armies joined up near Nantwich. Derby then moved his forces to Preston.

The legendary Colonel Robert Lilburne – one of the signatories on King Charles I's Death Warrant – hearing of the uprising in Lancashire, moved to Wigan expecting to find Derby's forces in the town, but they had left. He then moved towards Preston and engaged with Derby's forces in an inconclusive skirmish before Derby headed south once again towards Wigan. His plan was to move south to join up with the King's forces at Worcester, but it was not to be. Riding with him at the head of his forces was General Sir Thomas Tyldesley, whose Royalist loyalties demonstrated an almost apostolic zeal!

But Derby had an army which did not work as a well-disciplined unit. Derby's forces were catholic and Anglican, but the Scots were staunchly Calvanist. They were fighting in the hope that the new king would keep his promise of declaring Presbyterianism as the official religion – at least in Scotland but, they hoped, nationally – and had little time for, and considerable mistrust of, Derby's followers.

By lunchtime on 25 August 1651, they had covered almost all of the eighteen miles to Wigan; they had passed the Boar's Head Inn and were less than a mile from the centre of the town when Lilburne's forces, who had been concealed in the woodlands, revealed themselves on the hillside above the River Douglas. As most seventeenth-century battles were set-piece affairs, he probably felt there was a greater chance of a convincing defeat in a full-scale battle, than that which might result from an ambush.

Roundhead intelligence had been forewarned of the Royalists' approach – in fact every move Derby had made since landing near present-day Pressall had been reported back to Cromwell who was reportedly encamped with his armies near Manchester.

The battle which ensued was the last battle of the Civil Wars to take place in Lancashire, and arguably one of the most important. The Royalists, hugely outnumbered, could not contemplate either defeat or retreat, yet knew their chances of victory was slim. Undaunted, Derby and Tyldesley marshalled their troops and prepared for action, but as the battle unfolded, they were pushed steadily northwards, back towards Standish.

Derby had undoubted courage, but little strategic know-how, and even knowing that defeat was becoming increasingly likely, he remained in the thick of the battle, suffering several wounds as a result. Around him his soldiers were dying in their hundreds – indeed very heavy losses were incurred on both sides – and many of his troops fled from the inevitable outcome. In less than two hours half of the Royalists were dead, and a further third were taken prisoner. Amongst the mortally wounded was Lord Widdrington – whose name is remembered in one of the town's streets – and Sir Thomas Tyldesley was dead.

When all seemed lost, Derby fled with his surviving officers and a few men, and surprisingly made his way to a safe house in Wigan rather than heading north to obvious safety. His plan seems always to have been to join up with the King, and this he eventually did at Worcester. While in Wigan, his wounds were treated by a local publican in the Old Dog Tavern in the Market Place.

Lilburne wrote his account of the battle in a letter to Robert Birch, the Roundhead military commander of Liverpool that night and it was delivered on 26 August.

He wrote:

Honoured Sir,
The Lord hath pleased this day, to appear for us, in the total rout and overthrow of the Lord of Derby and his force, which was increased to about 1500. He himself, though wounded, escaped, though narrowly. I

The Old Dog, Market Place, from an 1826 painting by Thomas Whitehouse. Whitehouse wrote on this painting that the Old Dog was 'where the Earl of Derby was concealed after his defeat at the Battle in Wigan Lane'.

would only entreat you to send out what horse you have or can get, to ride up and down the country to gather up stragglers. I cannot enlarge myself at present, but entreat you to accept this from him that desires to express himself. Your ammunition is come safe. The Lord of Derby I hear is fled towards Bolton, but his sumptures and treasure is here. We intended for Manchester this night, and had hopes to take my Lord General's regiment of foot, and to have five hundred men in readiness to join them. The Lord Widdrington cannot live long. Colonel Boynton and Tyldesley are slain. I have diverse other colonels prisoners. Your very humble servant, Robert Lilburne.

Derby surrendered after the Battle of Worcester, and was subsequently tried for treason and executed at Bolton – his execution supervised by Alexander Rigby, Wigan's Member of Parliament. The scaffold was, according to tradition, built using wood taken from Debry's estates around Lathom House. His body lay overnight in Wigan before being taken to Lathom House and onto Ormskirk Churchyard for burial. The charges against him were based on his Royalist sympathies – and he was held responsible for the massacre in Bolton in 1644, making Bolton an emotive choice for his place of execution.

Twenty-eight years later, in 1679, another Alexander Rigby, faithful Cornet, or standard bearer to Sir Thomas Tyldesley, paid for a monument to be erected in memory of Tyldesley on the spot at which he fell during the Battle of Wigan Lane.

Long before the end of the war, Wigan's fortunes had deteriorated to a disastrous level, as a 1649 petition recounts:

> The hand of God is evidently seen stretched out upon the county, chastening it with a three-corded scourge of sword, pestilence and famine, all at once afflicting it. They have borne the heat and the burden of a first and second war in an especial manner . . . In this county hath the playe of pestilence been ranging these three years and upwards, occasioned chiefly by the wars. There is a very great scarcity and dearth of all provisions, especially of all sorts of grain, particularly that kind by which that county is most sustained, which is full sixfold the price that of late it hath been. All trade, by which they have been much supported, is utterly decayed; it would melt any good heart to see the numerous swarms of begging poore, and the many families that pine away at home, not having faces [i.e. being too proud] to beg.

With the war over, the town slowly rebuilt itself and its industry, but it was a slow process, for the industrial and trading infrastructure of the country as a whole was deflated.

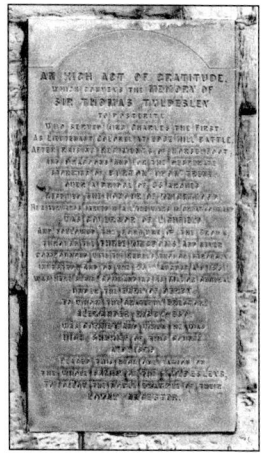

The Tydesley Monument on Wigan Lane remembers the heroics of Sir Thomas during the Battle of Wigan Lane. Nearby is Widdrington Road, named after Lord Widdrington who also died at the battle.

A halfpenny trading token, issued by Wigan merchant Thomas Cooper in 1666. It was not uncommon for merchants in the seventeenth century to pay their employees with tokens which could only be spent in the company store.

By 1653, Cromwell had dispensed with the Rump Parliament and was ruling with the support of a group of advisors. He continued so to do until his death on 3 September 1658, the seventh anniversary of the pivotal Battle of Worcester at which the Royalists had finally been defeated. He had nominated his son Richard as his successor just before his death, but was immediately at odds with the army, which wanted a republic to be declared.

A few months later Richard Cromwell resigned and the army's first act was to restore the Rump Parliament – and thus in 1659 Wigan's two Puritan members Hugh Forth and Robert Markland made their way once again to London.

The republic idea came to nothing, and late in the year King Charles II, whom the Royalists had recognised as King since 1649, returned to Britain to widespread acclamation.

The King called a 'Convention' rather than a Parliament in 1660 – effectively summonsing those members elected but purged back in 1648 – but it lasted a very short period of time before being replaced by what became known as the Cavalier Parliament. The electoral confusion which followed in the borough demonstrates just how far allegiances had moved since the war – for Wigan submitted two pairs of 'duly elected' members. One pair was the Puritan High Forth together with William Gardiner, while the others were the staunch Anglicans and Monarchists John Molyneux and Roger Stoughton. The elections were declared void and a new ballot held, won the second time by Stoughton and Molyneux, who represented the town until the parliament was dissolved at Christmas.

The following year a series of acts were introduced to rid the church of Dissenters, and many clergy chose poverty rather than conform to the new requirements of the Church of England. One of the disbarred clergy, Charles Hotham, was eventually ejected from Wigan Hall in 1662 and replaced by George Hall – whose incumbency had been proposed by none other than Sir Orlando Bridgeman, back in favour again after his effective banishment from public life in 1642.

King Charles II's 1662 Charter – Wigan's eleventh royal charter – was perhaps the borough's most significant.

That 1660 Parliament was the first at which political labels started to be widely attached to candidates. During the Commonwealth, candidates had started to align with political groupings and the public became familiar with the terms 'Whigs' and 'Tories'. After the restoration, the Tory name became more closely associated with the monarchists, while the Whigs – taking their name from a Scottish Presbyterian movement – were dedicated to the expansion of parliamentary power and were, initially at least, drawn from the Presbyterian and Puritan religious movements.

When Sir Roger Bradshaigh was first elected as a member for Wigan in 1679 it was as a Tory, but his son – also Sir Roger – after gaining election as a Tory, became a staunch Whig and served the people of Wigan from 1698 until his death in 1746!

The restored King, keen to show appreciation to the borough that had served him so loyally, issued a charter in 1662 granting the burgesses and the corporation wide-reaching powers. In the charter, the Commonwealth is referred to only as 'in the late calamitous times!' As well as confirming all the earlier charters, the King granted the borough corporation much wider-reaching powers than those which had been enjoyed hitherto. As ever in charters, the language is tortuous:

> . . . Know ye therefore that we, graciously desiring the improvement of the borough aforesaid, and the prosperous condition of our people there, and revising and taking in good part the many and great services so seasonably bestowed by that borough to our Most Serene Father of blessed memory in the late most calamitous times, and also the continued fidelity and exceeding willing affection of the inhabitants of the same borough towards us and for our service, of our special grace and of our certain knowledge and mere notion have willed, ordained, granted, and confirmed, and by these present for ourselves, our heirs, and successors do will, ordain, grant, and confirm to the aforesaid mayor, bailiffs and burgesses of the borough aforesaid and their successors, the aforesaid body corporate, and all manner of liberties, free customs, immunities, exemptions, easements and jurisdiction, and hereditaments whatsoever which the burgesses of the vill or borough of Wigan aforesaid, or which the burgesses and community of the vill or borough of Wigan aforesaid, or which the mayor, bailiffs and burgesses of the vill or borough of Wigan aforesaid, and their predecessors whomsoever, by whatever names they were rated or called, or by whatsoever name or incorporation or pretence of whatsoever incorporation they have heretofore been incorporated, lawfully had, held, used or enjoyed . . . by reason or pretence of any charters or letters patent by us or any of our progenitors . . . by these presents in form aforesaid, confirmed in such ample manner and form

to all intents and purposes, as in times past they have had, held, used or enjoyed ... and confirm to our beloved Roger Bradshaigh, Knight, now the mayor of that borough of Wigan aforesaid, to be and continue mayor of that borough for and during the accustomed time of his continuing in that office, according to the use and custom within that borough in that behalf in times past accustomed ...

While confirming all the rights and privileges contained in earlier charters, King Charles II's charter also required anyone aspiring to hold civic office to swear the Oath of Obedience and the Oath of Supremacy. He also extended to the burgesses, bailiffs and people of the town the right to own, buy and sell land capable of yielding an annual rent up to a value of £50. The most significant as far as the town was concerned was the right to hold a 'Pie-Powder Court'. Now, for a town of Wigan's trading importance, this was a significant right, for it gave the magistrates of the town the right to hear cases relating to minor offences committed by non-residents. Wigan had, for centuries, had the authority to hold Courts Leet, to hear cases relating to its own residents, but had very limited jurisdiction relating to outsiders visiting the town. The Pie Powder Court – a corruption of the french *pied-poudre* meaning dusty feet – specifically related to offences committed during the many markets and fairs which brought so many travellers into the town. Apparently, the town made a significant income from fines levied through this court!

The unpopular Duke of York, as James II, succeeded his brother to the throne in 1685, despite several attempts by the Commons to bar him, and in the elections that year Wigan voted staunchly Tory.

The last – and incredibly long and detailed – charter of the seventeenth century was issued by King James II in 1685 established twelve Aldermen in the borough, who would form the Common Council, and in so doing, gave royal approval to the Corporation as the ruling body of the borough, able to pass byelaws and other local ordinances. By so doing, the modern structure of local government in the town was established in time for the new century.

King James II's Charter from February 1685 continued the style of incorporating the monarch's portrait within the initial letter. It was this Charter that established the Town's 'Common Council'.

CHAPTER 6
The Eighteenth-Century Industrial Town

James II, the younger son of Charles I, reigned for only four years after becoming King, before fleeing to France in 1689 amidst growing discontent over his pro-Catholic stance. A Catholic himself, he sought to remove the many laws which had excluded Catholics from universities, the judiciary and a whole raft of other areas of public life. His reign was almost immediately punctuated by a series of rebellions, and an appalling series of miscarriages of justice and executions under the infamous Judge Jeffries.

William III and Mary II became the joint rulers by invitation – Mary was James' daughter but not the immediate heir to the throne as James had a son by his second wife Mary of Modena. That son, later known as the Old Pretender, would become the figurehead of the Jacobite rebellions which dominated the first half of the eighteenth century.

But long before then, there were several attempts to restore James II to the throne, one of which was master-minded at Standish Hall over Christmas 1689. A group of local men gathered at Standish over Christmas and New Year, all swearing an oath of secrecy, knowing that if their plot became public knowledge, they would all be tried for treason. But, despite all their efforts, there was a spy in their midst!

Religion was, of course, at the core of the plot. The Catholic families of Lancashire were incensed by the enthronement of the Protestant William and Mary while there was a Stuart male with a much stronger claim to the throne – James II's son, the Catholic Prince James. Lancashire was still a Catholic stronghold, as well as being a Stuart stronghold. The plotters planned to raise funding and arms to be handed over to the rightful heir when he set foot on British soil again, believing that he would then move south towards London with an increasingly powerful army. Had they succeeded, the entire history of the British monarchy would have been changed, and but for one Robert Dodsworth, they might have seen their plans bear fruit.

William Standish hosted the meeting, and amongst the families represented were the Tyldesleys, the Stanleys, the Townleys, the Daltons of Thurnham, the Gerards of Bryn, several military figures, and representatives of the outlawed Catholic clergy.

Dodsworth had been invited to the meeting on account of his fervent Jacobite sympathies, but he was, in fact, on the payroll of King William.

The political and religious conflicts of the time can be seen in the family splits which once again became evident. While William Standish was plotting against William and Mary, his kinsman, Sir Richard Standish, Bart, was the Whig member of parliament for Wigan borough!

Almost as soon as decisions were made at Standish Hall, they were known about at court! As a result, William and Mary issued a strongly worded proclamation naming thirty-six of the plotters and warning of severe penalties for them if they were caught, and for anyone found to have aided, supported or hidden them. But, in the late seventeenth century, with transport and communication notoriously undependable, Dodsworth coup was the exception rather than the rule and, a year later,

William and Mary's 1690 Proclamation against William Standish and the other known plotters.

not one of the plotters had been arrested. Indeed William Standish had fled for a year but, by early 1692, was back at his home, and plotting another uprising!

His second attempt at overthrow was just as unsuccessful. This time he was betrayed by the two men to whom he entrusted the task of building up the stockpile of weapons at Standish Hall – John Womball and John Lunt.

The second plot was rather more ambitious – the plan called for King William to be assassinated to ease the return of James II! For the second plot, many of the original families had been joined by the Dicconsons, the Cliftons and others – yet William's warrant named only Standish, who had fled by that time, taking all the arms with him.

Several of the plotters were captured, and a number of notable trials were held, but all the charges were eventually dropped and the plotters freed. There was a suggestion that the evidence against them was so circumstantial that the King felt that to proceed with the charges would actually make martyrs out of the plotters and further their cause.

In an ironic twist, the evidence which might have sealed the fate of Standish and his fellow plotters was dug up by workmen on the Standish estate 250 years later, enabling historians to confirm that the plots had been clear in their intent, and the charges against the plotters well founded!

While all this plotting was going on around the periphery of the borough, the town itself was moving strongly forward on industrial and commercial fronts. The town's infrastructure, however, had not been moved forward at the same rate – and a number of contemporary accounts from travellers passing through the town in the early years of the eigteenth century include comments about the poor quality of the roads. The 'well-pavid' Wigan referred to by John Leland in 1540 was, by 1700, apparently a thing of the past.

In spite of the poor road systems, Wigan was still an attractive place to visit – in addition to the fairs and markets, as popular as ever, sporting events had been added, drawing a large entry to the town. In the *London Gazette* of 10 June 1700, such an event was advertised:

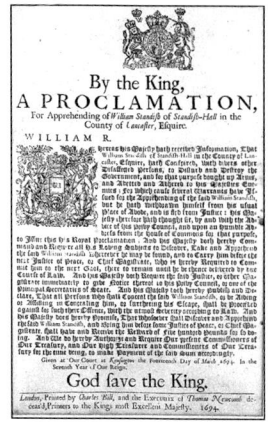

King William issued this 1694 Proclamation against William Standish after his second failed plot. Queen Mary had died earlier that same year.

> A plate of £10 value will be run for by footmen, on Tuesday, the 6 August next, at Wigan, in Lancashire, the usual 3 Miles Course there; all persons may run that enter their names with the Bayliffs there by the First of the said month, and that pays down 5s. On the 7th a Plate of 50s value will be run for there, excluding any as ran for the first Plate. And on the 8th a Plate of £5 value will be run for there, and any Persons to put in without paying anything to this or the foregoing Plate (except the winner of the first Plate), provided they enter their names to the above said.

From the Jacobite period in Wigan come these two treasures – a filligree writing case and a locket reputed to contain a lock of the hair of James III, the Old Pretender.

A prize value of £10 in 1700 must have been close to a prince's ransom, and such races must have been keenly competitive.

William III was succeeded to the throne by Queen Anne – during whose reign the English and Scottish Parliaments were united to create the United Kingdom – and, on her death in 1714, George, Elector of Hanover was proclaimed King. The Lancashire families who had opposed William and Mary were equally opposed to George I, and in 1715 a secret meeting took place in Wigan at John Shaw's Club. Loyalties within the town were, as ever, divided. When the uprising came about, the Jacobite armies moved south into Lancashire, declared James III King. Many local men moved north to join them and some, on entering Wigan – a town known to support the incumbent monarch – they robbed several locals, and damaged local property.

The Hanoverian armies under General Carpenter passed through Wigan heading north – linking up with Dragoons who had been stationed in the town along with general Stanhope's regiment of cavalry – and engaged the Jacobites in battle near Preston. All that most Wiganers saw of the Jacobite soldiers was them being led through the town in chains on their way south to London. Five local sympathisers – James Blindell, James Burn, John Finch, John Macillwray and William Whatley – were tried for treason at Preston Assizes and brought back to their native Wigan for public execution in the Market Place. Their execution was, reportedly, accompanied by enthusiastic cheers from the 'loyalists' and sympathetic groans from the Jacobite supporters amongst the crowd which had turned out to watch.

Thirty years later, this time behind the standard of the Young Pretender – Charles Edward Stuart, better known as Bonnie Prince Charlie – local men again rallied to the Jacobite cause. The armies recruited heavily in Manchester and Wigan, and moved south towards Derby. They were only saved from a bloody defeat by intelligence which warned them of a huge force waiting for them and commanded by generals Cumberland and Wade. They chose the wise option and retreated north again through Manchester and Wigan, their numbers depleting along the way as disillusioned followers returned to their homes and their occupations. Their cause would finally be snuffed out with the bloodiest battle of them all – Culloden.

Wiganers returned to their coal mining, their pewtering and the many other occupations which had become established in the town. They did not know it, of course, but the town was about to enter a period of rapid modernisation and industrialisation which would lay the foundations for the huge expansion which took place in the nineteenth century.

That expansion started in 1720, with two Acts of Parliament to enable the complete overhaul of the roads system approaching the town. One act covered the road north to Preston, while the other authorised the relaying of the road south to Warrington. For a town of Wigan's importance to have let the roads get into such a condition may well reflect the damage which had been done to its economy in the strife which had rumbled since the time of the Civil Wars. The 1720 Act noted that 'by reason of the many carriages of goods and merchandise passing through the same [the roads] are become ruinous and almost impassable, especially in the winter season, and some parts thereof are so narrow that coaches and carriages cannot pass by one another.'

The upkeep of roads was generally funded by tolls, and the roads leading in and out of Wigan were no exception. At the limits of the borough, there would have been toll gates – bars – to identify where the town's authority ended and the turnpike roads began. In the eighteenth century, burgesses and merchants could pass toll-free along the roads controlled by the Common Council, as long as they made a formal request so to do, in advance of their journeys.

With a huge increase in commercial and mining activity – and an increase in the materials being transported from Wigan to other towns – good roads were, doubtless, becoming a necessity.

Mining especially was on the increase. In addition to the Bradshaigh mines at Haigh and the many pits being developed closer to the town, the Dicconson family developed several mines in the Shevington area in the first half of the eighteenth century. They also developed coking ovens in Shevington at about this time – the remains of an early eighteenth-century oven were unearthed when the M6 was being built in the 1960s. The coking of coal had been known in England since the early sixteenth century, and had primarily been used to drive off the sulphur and create

The 'New Town Hall' in a prominent position in Market Place was completed in 1720. By the time this picture was taken in the 1870s, it was in a very poor condition. A row of butchers shops occupied the ground floor.

a sweeter-burning fuel. In Wigan, with the clean burning cannel in ready supply, such a process would not have been used for domestic purposes, so it is reasonable to assume that the coke was being produced to supply the town's iron foundries.

Coal was mined as well as cannel, and was the essential fuel for a whole range of local industries in the mid-eighteenth century – including bell-founders, brass-workers, pewterers, brick-makers, ceramists (using locally available clay for a time) glass-makers and ironfounders – and there are records of substantial amounts being exported to fuel industrial concerns in other towns.

The list of charges and exemptions for users of the Preston to Wigan toll road in 1720 gives a hint as to the scale of mining north of the town – specifically excluding from the toll charges 'any horses, geldings or mares, mules or asses, going to or returning from any coal pit.' There must have been significant traffic of that nature for there to be such specific exclusions. Many of the mines at that time would have been drift mines, with sloping roads offering a relatively gentle incline down to the coal face. The ponies and horses at that time were brought to the surface each day, and presumably brought back to stabling nearer the town. A century later, some ponies would spend their entire working lives in the total darkness of the deep mines, with underground stables provided for them.

The toll roads had their first major rival when the Douglas Navigation was completed in the 1740s, offering the potential of larger-capacity water-transport for the heavier and bulkier products of the town.

The Act of Parliament facilitating the Douglas Navigation was passed in the same year as that permitting road improvements – 1720 – and was titled *An Act for making the River Douglas (alias Asland) navigable from the River Ribble to Wigan* and was passed seven years after a similar proposal

It is hard to imagine that this river was, for a time, the main means of transport for Wigan's coal. Opened in 1742 after ten years' work, the Douglas Navigation linked the town's industries with the sea. A quay near Miry Lane marked the inland limits of the navigable stretch of the river. In the distance is the JJB Stadium.

had been rejected by the House of Lords. The proposal was to render the river navigable from its confluence with the Ribble, to a point near Miry Lane, only a few hundred yards from Wigan town centre.

Commissioners were appointed to oversee the works, and supervise the use of the river, and they included Edward Holt of Wigan, Hugh Holme of Holland House, Robert and William Bankes of Winstanley, Sir Roger Bradshaigh of Haigh, 3rd Baronet, and after his death in 1747, his son Roger, 4th Baronet – all of them colliery owners. From the outset, the primary purpose of the navigation was the transport of coal, and there are records from the earliest days of the navigation of substantial quantities of coal being loaded on to bow-hauled boats – hauled by gangs of men – and occasionally horse-drawn barges at Pool Bridge between Miry Lane and Newtown. Sir Roger Bradshaigh in 1743, for example, paid one John Pearson £4 10s for carting one thousand baskets of cannel coal from Haigh to the river.

The Douglas in those days was a very different river to today's narrow waterway, and was full of fish. Indeed indentured apprentices working in a factory near Adam Bridge 'were not to be fed Douglas salmon more than once a week'!

Work started on the project in 1732 and Alexander Leigh was paid the princely sum of 63 guineas per year for his work. He only claimed it periodically, and at the end of the project, submitted a bill for the previous four and a half years!

The banks of the river were shored with local wood and stone, and the weirs and locks were made of ash and fir, felled throughout the area. Records exist of timbers being brought to the river bank from woods in Shevington, Parbold, Wrightington, Bamfurlong and Harrock Woods. But while there was considerable enthusiasm for building the waterway, there seems to have been rather less commitment to maintaining it, and it was constantly having to be repaired.

From Dean Locks at Gathurst the river became tidal, and at that point many of the cargoes were trans-shipped to larger boats and carried to Tarleton. In addition to coal, the boats carried slate from Roby Mill, iron, and bricks from Wigan factories, and on the return journey they brought stone for local building projects, kelp for use in glass-making, and flax and cotton to supply the textile industries.

The entire project had cost £20,000 by the time it was completed, and it can hardly have been in profit when even greater plans were drawn up. Within thirty years of the completion of the Douglas Navigation it had reached almost the limit of its cargo-carrying capacity. The main restriction was the size of the boats – about 30ft long and about 6ft wide. As the output of the mines increased, larger craft were needed, and discussions started on the planning for the Leeds-Liverpool Canal.

Basket pits, where baskets where used to lower the miners and raise the coal, were a common sight in the second half of the eighteenth century. This example, at Winstanley, survived for over a century – long enough to be photographed c.1880.

The once quiet Douglas Valley now plays host to two hundred and fifty years of transport systems – the Douglas Navigation from 1742, the Leeds-Liverpool Canal from 1779, the nineteenth-century Lancashire and Yorkshire Railway and the 1960s M6 motorway. All four pass within a few yards of each other at Dean Locks near Gathurst.

By the second half of the eighteenth century, coal mines were getting deeper – with some pits using vertically sunk shafts instead of the more common drift mines – and pit head gear started to become a common sight on the skyline. The early pits used baskets to lower the miners and raise the coal.

Deeper and bigger mines produced more coal – hence the need for more effective systems of transportation. When the canal was opened, those lengths of it which could take standard-sized barges – from Liverpool to Wigan, Wigan to Leigh and Rufford to Tarleton – offered a huge increase in carrying capacity. The long boat had an overall length of 72ft – only 20 per cent longer than the Douglas 'flats', but their beam was 14.5ft, and their capacity several times greater. The fate of the Douglas Navigation was effectively sealed when the first stretches of the canal opened in 1779, but Alexander Leigh had sold his interests in the waterway to the Leeds & Liverpool Canal Company eight years earlier in 1771 for £14,500.

The canal's route ran parallel to the river for large stretches, so the network of tramways which had been put in place to deliver coal to the river boats required little modification to connect with the new canal. The advent of the canal brought huge benefits to late eighteenth-century Wigan, and even greater benefits in the century that followed.

In a town becoming increasingly renowned for mining and heavy industry, the quality of the pewter ware, the clocks and the watches being produced in the town in the second half of the eighteenth century is remarkable.

By the 1760s, Wigan was second only to London for the quality of its pewter, and Wigan watches were considered to be of very fine quality indeed.

Leaders amongst the town's eighteenth-century pewterers were the Bancks family, who owned extensive property in Market Plate, Standishgate

In the early years of the twentieth century, visitors to Wigan could choose from well over 100 different postcards of the town. This early coloured multi-view card dates from about 1908.

An early tinted postcard of Market Place, showing the single track narrow gauge rails for the steam trams which had been introduced in the 1870s. Near the hut on the right was a water hydrant from which the locomotives' boilers could be filled.

Looking up Wallgate from the canal basin towards the railway bridge, about 1910, as a single-deck tram to Pemberton makes it way down the street. 'Wigan looks fair today' says the message on the postcard, 'but give me Somerset!'

The top of Wallgate, looking down towards the railway stations, seen from the Library Street corner c.1910. This was a favourite view for Edwardian postcard photographers, and at least a dozen variants on this scene – some in sepia, several tinted like this one – were on sale in the years before the Great War.

This early twentieth-century view from the top of Standishgate shows a single track electric tramline running down into the town centre. It was taken before Mab's Cross was moved across the road to its present site.

Standishgate from the Market Place, photographed just before the start of the Great War. Parked in the shadows on the left is an early steam-powered lorry, once a familiar sight on British roads. The open-fronted tramcar, No.73, manufactured by Dick Kerr and introduced in 1907, had probably made its way from Standish.

Wigan Coal & Iron Co.'s huge ironworks employed considerable numbers of local people, and consumed vast quantities of locally mined coal. The works are seen here on an early twentieth-century postcard.

The Pit Brow Lasses of Wigan's many collieries featured on many locally produced postcards. These strong Amazonian women screened and graded the coal as it passed by on huge conveyor belts, removing the stone and rubble.

This scene, from a hand-tinted postcard c.1904, was typical of a hundred locations in the Wigan area in the heyday of the mining industry – the dayshift leaving the pit head as the evening sunlight warmed the normally bleak surroundings.

Chisnall Hall Colliery near Coppull was the last of the Wigan Coal Corporation's pits to cease production when the NCB closed it in 1968. When this picture was taken in 1974, work to restore the site had not yet started.

Alfred Waterhouse's fine Public Library building – 125 years old in 2003 – is now the History Shop and stages local exhibitions in the former Lending Library. Upstairs, the Reading Room has been preserved largely as it was in 1878.

The Haigh Steam and Vintage Fair, held over the three-day August Bank Holiday weekend, has become an annual event in the Wigan calendar. Here two musicians entertain visitors to the 2001 event.

Above: After having made its way up the Wigan flight of locks from the Pier basin, a boat passes under Bridge 57 at Top Lock in the late 1970s. The owners of many of today's narrowboats have had them painted in more traditional designs.

Below: Winter sunlight reflects off a group of houseboats tied up along the towpath on the Leeds-Liverpool Canal near the Crawford Arms at Red Rock. Today the canal is almost exclusively used by privately-owned narrowboats and cruisers.

History & Guide

Above: The 'Indestructible Ventilating Fan' was manufactured at Pagefield Iron Works by Walker Brothers (Wigan) Ltd, and used to ventilate coal mines not just in Wigan but throughout the world. These huge fans could drive almost a million cubic feet of air per minute down into Wigan's hot and humid deep mines.

Left: The world's largest working steam engine can be seen in the engine house at Trencherfield Mill, part of the Wigan Pier Heritage Centre. The mill was built in the early twentieth century, the last mill in Wigan to be built near a canal rather than a railway, and had its own canal cutting.

Right: *Lindsay is the last surviving example of the steam locomotives manufactured at the Kirkless Works of the Wigan Coal & Iron Co. These powerful little locomotives worked the coal wagons in the company's many pits.* Lindsay *was rescued from certain destruction in the 1970s and, thanks to a painstaking restoration, was back in steam to celebrate her 100th birthday in 1987. A commemorative brass plaque was fixed to the locomotive to mark the occasion. She is seen here pulling a visitor train in 1987 on the short track at Steamtown, the now-closed steam preservation centre at Carnforth.*

Below: *Since 1949, Wigan and District Model Engineering Society has operated a miniature steam railway at Haigh Hall – seen here in use in the early 1980s. A few years after this picture was taken the track was considerably extended.*

Published by James Valentine of Dundee c.1912, this rare view shows Mesnes Street looking towards Bridgeman Terrace and Rylands' Mill in the distance. Holcroft's Tavern – later the Market Tavern – is on the left, with Hope Church beyond.

For a time in the early 1980s, while work progressed on the Galleries, the outdoor market stalls which had previously been set up in Woodcock Street at the top end of the old Market Hall were moved to a temporary site in New Market Street.

The Pavilion in Mesnes Park with its cast-iron canopies and lantern roof – seen here in a view after snow in late 1969 – was designed as the focal point of the park and completed in time for the opening by the High Sheriff of Lancashire in 1878.

Standishgate in 1999, traffic free for most of the day, and lined with trees. Shortly after this picture was taken the roadway was paved, but over the years the bustle which once typified Wigan's main shopping street has diminished considerably.

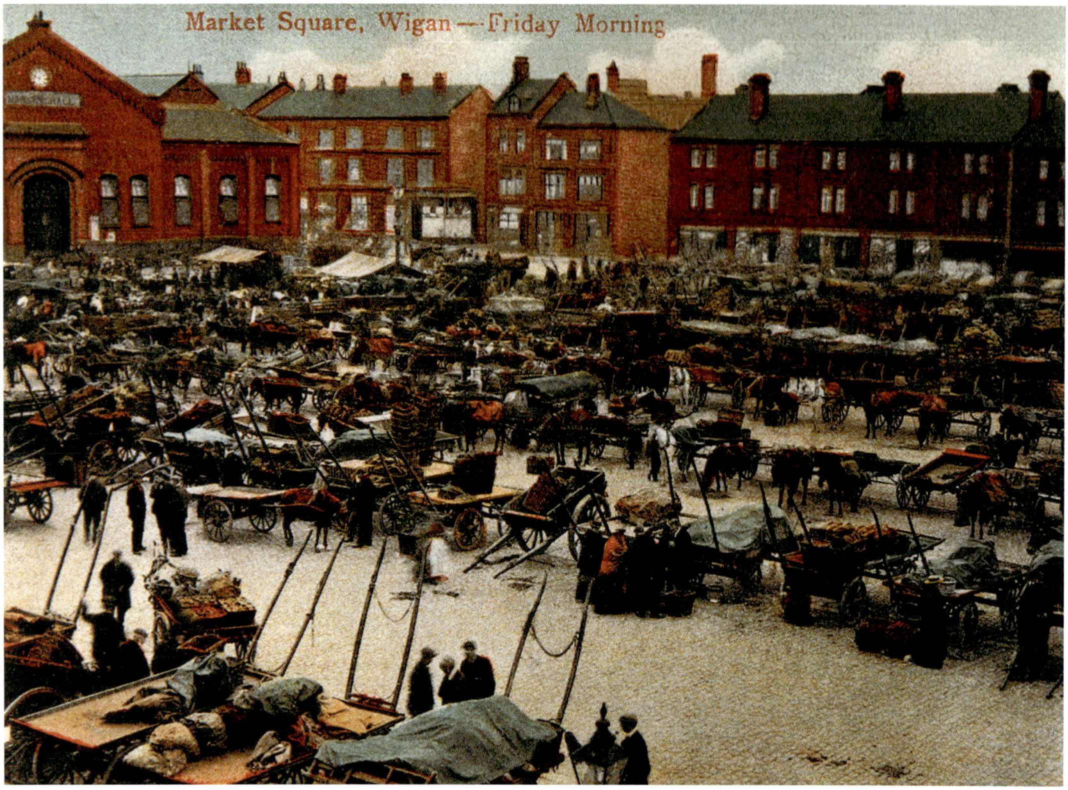
Market Square, Wigan — Friday Morning

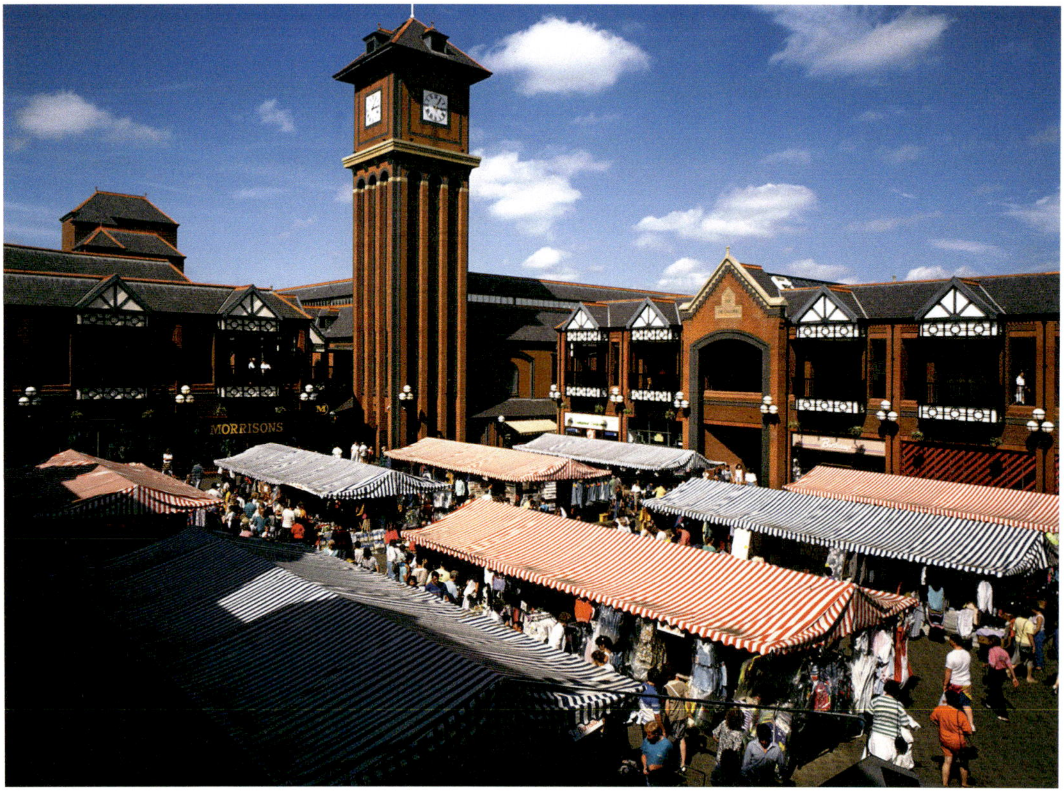
MORRISONS

Above: *Wigan's Victorian Market Hall celebrated its centenary in 1977, but very shortly afterwards, decisions were made to demolish it and replace it with today's Galleries Shopping Centre. Opened in 1877, it was extended first to provide a fresh fish market and covered fruit and vegetable stalls, and later to incorporate a row of shops on the Market Street side. This photograph, dating from about 1904, featured on an early postcard.*

Left: *The stallholders in the old market hall offered a much wider range of merchandise than can now be found in the new building. This photograph of a pot stall in the old market hall photographed was taken in the early 1980s, less than three years before the building was demolished.*

Opposite page: *Eighty years separate these two pictures of Wigan's Market Square. The upper picture was taken c.1904, the lower one in 1987 shortly after the Galleries opened. Since then, the striped awnings have been replaced with utilitarian plastic roofs.*

Thirty years ago Haigh Hall still had a beautiful lily pond, and hot houses filled with unusual and exotic flowers. When this picture was taken in 1970, the plant houses were still well cared for, but by the 1980s they had been allowed to fall into such disrepair that they had become a danger to visitors and were eventually demolished.

Over the past thirty-five years, Makinson's Arcades has been given several facelifts. When this picture was taken in 1986, before the galleries were built, Boots' store occupied a large proportion of one side.

These days it does not snow very often in Wigan, but when it does, the landscape offers some stunning views for photographers. This family walking their dog in late afternoon sunlight along the path that runs from the foot of Coppull Lane into Haigh Plantations, was photographed after a heavy snow fall in early 1981.

The electric waterbus Emma sails towards 'The Way We Were' Heritage Centre in spring 2003. The Museum closed its door finally in December 2007 after twehty-one years, as part of the Wigan Pier Quarter regeneration project. The building's future is unclear.

Above: *The Orwell Pub and restaurant at Wigan Pier, photographed in 1999 – one of the restored buildings which will be at the heart of the new Wigan Pier Quarter regeneration project, aimed at bringing a range of cultural, educational and leisure facilities to the area.*

In 1970, with the site totally derelict and in danger of collapse, it is not surprising that the local council thought that the buildings around the canal basin at Wigan Pier should either be demolished, or screened off from public view.

A dramatic 1986 view showing the Orwell at Wigan Pier – before the clock tower was built – and the terminal warehouse. It was taken early on a spring evening a few weeks after her Majesty the Queen officially opened the heritage centre – 'The Way We Were' – on the completion of a multi-million pound restoration of this important industrial site.

and Scholes, and watches from around the same period have been identified bearing the names of Archibald Coates and James Coates.

In surviving 'burghal petitions' recorded by the Court Leet, attention is drawn to the restrictive practices operating within the town – and the difficulties encountered by anyone wishing to settle and work in Wigan. It would seem that the Council in the eighteenth century operated a severe system of fines and penalties for anyone living and working within the town without a permit, and for anyone harbouring a 'fariner' or foreigner.

One freeman was fined for allowing 'travelers' to lodge in his house without a permit 'so long as one bore a child.' In order to get permission to live and work in the town, there were elaborate – and expensive – protocols to be observed.

Even being able to demonstrate that there was work available was not enough in itself. Freedom to live and work in the borough came at a not inconsiderable price – a price which, apparently, varied according to the whim of the aldermen hearing the petition. One such petition reads:

Two eighteenth-century watches made in Wigan by James Coates and Archibald Coates.

> To the Worshipful John Markeland Esquire, Mayor of the Borough and Corporation of Wigan, in the County of Lancaster, and to the Aldermen and Jury assembled at the Court Leet held by adjournment in and for the said Borough, the 22nd day of January 1742.
>
> The humble petition of Thomas Chadwick, Linen weaver, Sheweth,– That your petitioner is in very good circumstances, has no family, and is desirous to inhabit and follow his Trade in your Corporation, and for that purpose to be admitted a freeman thereof, he be willing to pay such a sum of money for his freedom as your Worships and the Gentlemen of the Jury think proper.
>
> Your Petitioner, therefore, humbly prays you, Gentlemen of the Jury, that he may be admitted a freeman of this your Corporation, he paying such a sum of money for his freedom as your Worships and you, Gentlemen of the Jury, shall think proper.
>
> And your Petitioner shall ever pray. &c.
>
> We elect him a Freeman of this Corporation, he paying Four Pounds four shillings in a Month's time to the present bailiffs.

If such permission was not granted, the infiltrator could expect the wrath of the existing freemen to be ranged again him. At the same Court Leet, just such an incomer was accused:

> The Humble Petition of Richard Tyrer, Cooper, on behalf of himself and the rest of the Coopers' freemen of the said Borough, Sheweth, – That Peter Dykes, of Shevington, hath lately, without any right or authority whatsoever, come into your said Borough, and doth exercise

The Bancks family were Wigan's most celebrated pewterers in the seventeenth and eighteenth centuries, at a time when the reputation of the town's pewter was second only to London.

The elaborate French-style architecture of the NatWest Bank in Standishgate dates from c.1870, but there has probably been a bank on this site for 200 years.

and practice the Trade of a Hollow ware Turner in the said Borough, to the great detriment of your Petitioner and others, Freemen Coopers of this Corporation, and in defiance of the Laws of this Corporation.

The outcome of the petition was that the said Peter Dykes of Shevington was severely fined, and given thirty-eight days to cease trading, and informed that he would be fined thirty-nine shillings per month if he defied the court's judgement. A similar penalty was imposed on two tailors as a result of a petition from the Freemen Taylors. So freedom to work within the borough was backed up by a whole raft of local byelaws.

One of the area's most notable industrial facilities of the early nineteenth century – Haigh Foundry – started production in 1790 by the banks of the Leeds-Liverpool Canal. To facilitate the movement of materials in and out of the ironworks, a small basin was dug out by the canalside. By the early years of the nineteenth century, the superintendent of the foundry would be Robert Dalglish who would play a major part in introducing steam traction into the country.

As the eighteenth century drew to a close, the industrial and commercial strength of the borough was further underlined by the establishment of the Wigan Bank – the town's first – founded by Thomas Baldwin in 1792. The Baldwins had been a prominent family in the town since the mid-seventeenth century, owning extensive lands and properties. Just where the bank opened its first premises has not been discovered, but by the early the nineteenth century it had its offices at Bank House, No.4 Standishgate. By 1869, the name had been changed to Woodcock, Sons and Eckersley's Bank, and by 1890 it had become Parr's Bank. Over the subsequent century of takeovers and mergers it has become today's NatWest Bank, and still operates from that same address. That century would also see a massive expansion of Wigan's industry, and a huge increase in the town's population.

Haigh Foundry was one of the contractors appointed by Jesse Hartley to manufacture ironwork for Liverpool's Albert Dock. The swing bridges were designed by the famous engineer John Rennie, and built at Haigh in 1845. One example still survives today, spanning the dock entrance from the River Mersey.

CHAPTER 7
Victorian Wigan: Cotton, Coal and Railways

The nineteenth century dawned with King George III on the throne, William Pitt the younger as Prime Minister, and Britain at war with France and Spain.

The new century was the century of steam. Steam engines, which had hitherto been stationary devices, were given wheels, and the railway age was born.

Within a very few years of his appointment in charge of Haigh Ironworks, Robert Dalglish had secured the rights to build steam pumping engines, both to Newcomen designs and to those of Boulton and Watt. The use of steam pumping engines in Wigan mines had been introduced before 1790, and had revolutionised deep mining in the area. Wigan's deeper pits were always wet, as once the rock stratum above the coal seams had been penetrated, large quantities of water seeped into the workings. The Haigh Foundry soon found itself with full order books as the number of local mines increased. But Dalglish did not stop there – he foresaw the application of steam to the haulage of coal, and acquired the manufacturing rights for the Blenkinsop locomotive, a five-wheeled engine which was powerful enough to haul coal tubs along specially designed tramways. Modifying the design to improve traction and power – and renaming it the Dalglish Walking Horse, by 1812 he had produced the first steam locomotive to be seen in Lancashire, seven years before the opening of the Stockton & Darlington Railway.

Opinions differ on this picture – it is either an early photograph of a Dalglish/Blenkinsop locomotive pulling coal wagons along a tramway, or, more likely, of a model of the same.

The central wheel of the locomotive was the only one which was driven by the steam engine. It was toothed, connecting with protruding rods along the outer edge of one of the rails. This ensured that there was excellent traction with no slippage as the locomotive hauled its heavy load.

The first colliery to employ the new technology was the John Pit in Orrell, and the locomotive hauled tubs along the tramway between the pit and the Leeds-Liverpool Canal.

For the mine owners, steam power represented a cost saving once the initial outlay of the locomotives had been met. Where horse-drawn coal wagons required horses, stables, handlers, blacksmiths and feed, the 'walking horse' was fed with their own produce – coal.

Elsewhere, steam engines had been installed in mills and manufactories long before 1790, but Wigan was rather slow to adopt this technology. As far as the textile industry was concerned, most textile workers in Wigan still worked at home, using manually powered spinning and weaving equipment. The advent of the powerful steam engine, therefore, heralded the introduction of the textile mill and the beginning of the end for home weavers and spinners.

In Wigan steam was slow to make inroads into the cotton mills. By the start of the nineteenth century, while weaving was still a largely home-based activity, spinning mills – sometimes water-powered, but usually manually driven 'Jenny Mills' – had started to appear. Wigan had eight such mills by 1811 employing just over 600 people. Samuel Crompton's survey of the Wigan cotton industry in that year showed that the mills were still relatively small – most with a capacity of less than 2,500 spindles, and only one with more than 10,000. Wigan had fallen behind in many things by that time – textile capacity being no exception – and spinning mills with more than 25,000 spindles were already found

By the time this photograph of the huge Swan Meadow Mill complex was taken in the early 1920s, Eckersleys had had a cotton mill on this site for a century.

Throughout the expansion of the coal mining industry in the nineteenth century, all the shafts were dug by navvies with picks and shovels. This photograph shows the sinking of the Victoria Pit at the Boar's Head in the 1890s.

Carving in cannel coal was popular throughout the eighteenth and nineteenth centuries. This plaque is a likeness of Lord Lindsay.

in Bolton and other local towns. Manchester had steam-driven spinning mills by 1790!

The town started to catch up with the opening of Woods' and Rylands first mills in Wallgate in the early years of the century, the first Trencherfield Mill in the 1820s, and Eckersley's Swan Meadow Mill in 1822. All were steam powered.

Many of the new mill owners were former spinners or weavers who had invested wisely, seeing the potential of the new mass production methods. Several of them became very wealthy indeed.

By the mid-1830s, the employment profile of the town had changed out of all recognition. From a population of under 40,000 living within Wigan Parish, more than 7,500 men, women and children were employed in the textile industries – both handloom weavers working from home and those working in the town's twenty-one mills – 6,000 of them working in mills, up from only 600 less than twenty years earlier.

In addition, over fifty collieries were operating within the Wigan coalfields, employing approaching 10,000 people. Mines were, by that time, being sunk to depths of up to 800ft – a phenomenal achievement considering the shafts were sunk by navvies using nothing more than picks and shovels.

A gas works had been opened in 1823 and a waterworks a few years earlier – so the town was rapidly developing. Not as rapidly as its neighbours, though. In 1700, Wigan had been comparable in size with Manchester and Liverpool. By the 1830s, however, Manchester was over three times the size, and Liverpool, at 165,000, had almost four times Wigan's population.

The cast iron milepost at Boar's Head was restored in the 1990s, a century and a half after it was made at Haigh Foundry.

On 3 September 1832 an event of major significance took place – only two years after the opening of the Liverpool & Manchester Railway, the first passenger train left Wigan's Chapel Lane Station, and ran the few miles down to Parkside Station near Newton-le-Willows, where it met the L&M. Wigan had joined the railway age! Of course, long before then mineral lines had started to be developed, but the opening of a passenger link, albeit indirect, with the two major centres to east and west was an important event in the town's nineteenth-century development. Built at a cost of £70,000, the new railway was just the first of several lines in and out of the town. Between 1835 and 1838, a line was opened north to Preston, and the terminus at Chapel Lane was replaced by a new station on the site of today's North Western. A direct railway link with Manchester and Liverpool was achieved when Wallgate Station – on the Lancashire & Yorkshire Railway's line – was opened in 1848.

Photographers line the route as a steam special pulled by Jubilee Class 5XP locomotive Bahamas *leaves Wallgate Station in 1988 on its way to Southport.*

The L & YR route through the town was 150 years old when this photograph of Wallgate Station was taken in 1998. The present building at street level, however, dates from 1876, although at track level the station dates only from the 1970s.

The Illustrated London News *published this scene of strikers outside the Royal Hotel at the top of Standishgate during the 1853 industrial unrest.*

The Wigan Junction Railway, part of the Grand Central, built the third of the town's Victorian railway stations, Wigan Central, in 1892.

The huge progress in industrial output in the town in the first half of the nineteenth century had made many mill and mine owners very rich, but industrial relations were not good. By 1853, miners' earnings had risen very little in two decades, and the second half of the century was punctuated by a series of acrimonious industrial disputes.

In those days the miners were not paid wages as such, instead being treated almost as self-employed sub-contractors receiving 1s 5d (about 7p) per ton of coal mined. When their request for a raise of tuppence per ton was turned down, they withdrew their labour. They suffered more than their employers as a result, for if they did not work, they earned no money. Mine-owners' profits plummeted as well, but it was the workers, of course, who suffered the greatest hardship.

A scheduled protest march in the town on 4 November 1853 focused on the Royal Hotel where the mine owners were meeting, and turned nasty when troops were brought into the town from Manchester in support of the local police.

According to the *Illustrated London News* – in a typically understated manner:

> a great deal of damage was done to property and for four hours a mob held complete possession of the place . . . a meeting of mine owners took place in the Royal Hotel and when it broke up, several hundred miners had assembled hoping the masters would have compromised the dispute by consenting to give an advance of one penny to the shilling. When the men learned the masters had only decided to throw open their pits for the men to go to work at the same prices as they came out, they seemed much disappointed and showed an uneasy feeling.

Buildings were damaged in Queen Street, Market Place and Wallgate, market stalls were overturned, and it was only the intervention of the troops that restored some sort of order.

The order was short-lived, however, when rumours spread that Lord Crawford was planning to bring miners in from Wales to get his mines working again. Both Welsh and Irish miners were indeed brought in, reportedly put up in makeshift accommodation at New Springs, and put to work at Moor Pit – the fifth shaft at which had been sunk five years earlier. Eventually the dispute was settled in the miners' favour, but feelings ran high for some years.

In addition to the *Illustrated London News* coverage, the riots were reported in the newly established *Wigan Observer* which had started publication earlier in the year.

The miners' riots had not been the town's first – in the previous year, 1852, there had been riots in Scholes provoked by fighting between the Irish community and other residents, and although the cause of the unrest is unclear, considerable damage was done to an already impoverished area of the town. Before that, the town had experienced severe rioting as far back as 1819, and an earlier miners' strike over wages had taken place in 1831.

Between 1832 and 1836, the town had been granted three new charters by King William IV – the first since 1685 – and the Corporation Act which passed into law on 9 September 1835 established the administrative structure of the Victorian borough. The number of residents eligible to vote in local elections, however, still numbered substantially less than one thousand – and indeed had hardly grown in a century.

Little London was a small narrow close or 'yard' off Standishgate – one of many such streets throughout the Victorian town. Fresh water was supplied from a communal tap in the street.

Joseph Rylands' Gidlow Mills seen across Mesnes Park in a postcard published c.1910.

The first half of the century saw the construction of many of the town's major cotton mills – but the cotton famine which came about as a result of the American Civil War took a terrible toll on the town. By the early 1860s, over seven thousand textile workers had been laid off and were suffering extreme hardships. Wigan's cotton industry had, earlier in the century, become dependent upon American cotton rather than the Egyptian crop on which the industry had originally been built, and it proved impossible to purchase enough raw material from the former suppliers.

As quickly as the shortage had come about, it was reversed by the end of the war and the second half of the century was punctuated with the construction of even larger mills.

Most of the nineteenth-century mills were predominantly spinning mills – although some had both spinning and weaving facilities – whereas a century earlier most of the town's textile workers had been weavers.

By the middle of the 1860s, the textile workforce had peaked at around 9,000, and dropped by a thousand as the nineteenth century drew to a close. It would rise again substantially during the twentieth century.

To support the textile industry, there were a number of dye works in Millgate, bobbin-turners in Queen Street, and a number of spindle-makers and shuttle-makers in Scholes.

The local bobbin makers, however, were unable to meet demand, and the town's spinning mills purchased supplies from other makers in the Lake District and in Blackburn.

The earlier mills had all been built around Wallgate and the canal, but Joseph Ryland's 1868 Gidlow Mills were built alongside the railway, reflecting the growing importance of the railway for the carriage of freight.

The invoice for the construction of Rylands' huge mill in 1868 shows that the total cost was over £140,000.

The Prince of Wales opened the Royal Albert Edward Infirmary, on the outskirts of the Victorian town, in 1873. Beyond it were green fields and the Plantation Gates.

The scene at North Western Station after the horrifying crash in August 1873, as it appeared alongside a detailed report on the accident in the Illustrated London News.

In the same year as Ryland's Mill opened, the old Moot Hall in Market Place was demolished to make way for street improvements.

Elsewhere in the town, plans were already in hand to build a new hospital on Wigan Lane, and the Prince and Princess of Wales, later King Edward VII and Queen Alexandra, visited the town to perform the opening ceremony in 1873.

Very shortly afterwards, the new facilities were probably appreciated by the many casualties from the town's worst rail disaster in August 1873, when a night train was derailed as it passed through the station travelling at about forty miles an hour. Twelve passengers were killed and many more injured. They were treated as befitted their class – first class passengers were initially taken to the Royal Hotel, second class to the platform waiting room, while third class injured were treated on the open platform!

During their visit to open the infirmary, the Prince and Princess of Wales stayed with Lord Crawford at Haigh Hall, and his lordship was moved to name his new pit in Whelley after the princess – the Alexandra.

For their royal visitors, the Lindsays had Haigh Hall completely redecorated, and fitted out with new carpets and curtains at a cost of £80,000 – a very considerable expense a century and a quarter ago! The royal visit resulted in 150 servants and 50 policemen having to be found sleeping accommodation on the estate!

Elsewhere, ring spinning, which had been commonplace in American cotton mills since the 1830s, finally arrived in Wigan in the 1870s and started to replace the slower and bulkier mules. By the end of the nineteenth century, the town's mills would boast over one million ring spindles.

Ring spinning started to replace mule spinning in Wigan's mills in the 1870s, almost forty years after it had been pioneered in America. Mules took up much more floor space than ring spindles, the latter permitting much greater productivity on the spinning floor. The upper photograph shows mule spinning in Ryland's Mills near Mesnes Park, c.1910, while the lower photograph, dating from the 1950s, shows part of one of the ring spinning rooms at Eckersley's Swan Meadow Mills.

Mesnes Park was opened in 1878, about twenty-five years before this postcard view was published by Will Smith of Wigan Lane.

The 1870s saw the first large clothing factories open in the town, to join the many and varied other sources of employment for the expanding population. Largest and probably most important of these was Timothy Coop's whose fine building, opened in 1872, although no longer used for its original purpose, still dominates part of the skyline.

The major civic development in the town during the 1870s was undoubtedly the construction of the Market Hall, and the laying out of Market Square as a major public space. The Market Hall opened in 1877 and provided a covered and permanent venue for many of the stalls which had hitherto lined Market Place and the top of Standishgate. The Mayor, Alderman Mayhew, opened it with great civic ceremony. It was to serve the town for a few years over a century, before being demolished in the 1980s to make way for the Galleries Shopping Centre which also occupies the site of the Market Square. Another civic bash celebrated its centenary in 1977, and despite considerable public outcry, its demolition could not be halted.

A year after the Market Hall opened its doors, Mesnes Park opened its gates for the first time – formally opened by Nathaniel Eckersley, the High Sheriff of Lancashire at the time. The new park with its small serpentine lake was an oasis of green in an otherwise dark and sombre town. Industry was never far away, however, as the park was overlooked by Rylands' Mill at the top of the hill, and flanked on one side by the North Western Railway's line to London and Preston.

The nineteenth century had also been a period of intensive house-building to meet the needs of the growing workforce. As elsewhere, the housing being built was very basic, and the housing density considerable. The Scholes area had expanded enormously by the 1880s, as had the areas around Wallgate and the many cotton mills. Narrow closes and 'lands' off the main streets were lined with brick-built housing from the late eighteenth century, already in poor condition, and blackened by a century of soot from the smoke of thousands of domestic fires as well as the great steam engines powering the town's industry.

There were also, by then, almost 100 pits in the surrounding area employing, in addition to the miners, about 600 women on the coal screens, grading the coal and loading wagons – work they had been restricted to since women working underground had been outlawed in 1842. Pit girls chose the open air life rather than the damp and unhealthy cotton mills which employed about 90 per cent of the town's female workforce.

In the early 1890s, Central Station opened as the Wigan terminus of the Grand Junction Railway, but it was never a successful line. Not surprisingly, it did not survive the Beeching cuts of the 1960s.

As the century drew to a close, the Wigan coalfield was producing about five million tons a year – out of Lancashire's total of seven million – and the cotton industry was at its peak employing thousands of men and women. The town, while not the archetype of the soot-covered northern industrial town, cannot have been the most pleasant place to live and work.

Wigan Central Station had been open only a few years when this photograph was taken c.1900.

By 1964 Central Station had been closed, its wooden buildings and wooden platforms left to rot. For some years the station building was used by a builders' merchant, before it was demolished in the 1970s.

CHAPTER 8
Wigan in the Twentieth Century

Life in Wigan at the close of the nineteenth century must have been hard for the majority of Wiganers, but with relatively full employment – albeit at low wages – and huge expansion in both the textiles and mining industries, the town looked forward positively to the new century.

Queen Victoria's Diamond Jubilee was celebrated throughout the town – a town she never visited in all of her sixty-four years on the throne, although the Prince of Wales made his second visit in 1897. Four years later the Queen was dead, and the new King inherited not just the throne, but a country at war in South Africa.

The Boer Wars lasted from 1899 until 1902, and claimed the lives of quite a number of Wigan men from the 1st Volunteer Brigade of the Manchester Regiment. As a result, the town's first war memorial – the work of the eminent sculptor William Goscombe John (1860-1952) – was erected in 1903 in front of the pavilion in Mesnes Park. The bronze soldier stood on a stone plinth which remembered the 'Regular and Volunteer Imperial Yeomanry' who had fallen, many of them at the infamous Spion Kop.

Welsh-born Goscombe John had studied under Rodin in Paris in the 1890s, and Wigan's Boer Soldier was one of many fine public sculptures he created. It was removed for restoration in the 1960s and subsequently disappeared. What a pity it has been lost through civic neglect!

The Boer War Memorial in Mesnes Park, published as a postcard c.1910. The memorial was removed in the 1960s 'for restoration' and subsequently lost. As this book goes to press, there is talk, forty years later, of erecting a replacement. Group photographs taken on the pavilion steps always had the soldier, gun drawn, peering over the back row – as in this image, right, of the workforce at Bentley and Jubb's munitions factory during the First World War.

Hindley Fire Brigade placed a floral crown on their fire engine, and took part in the 1902 Coronation Parade.

A group of local school children presented an 'Empire Tableau' to mark the Coronation of King Edward VII in 1902.

In that same year, 1903, the new Mining and Technical College was opened in Library Street, replacing an earlier building on the site of today's International Pool. By the late 1980s, the building had been completely refurbished and reopened as Wigan Town Hall, giving the town an imposing town hall at last. Despite its long tradition as a borough, Wigan had not indulged itself in the nineteenth-century construction of a building which publicly advertised civic wealth and power in the manner of Bolton or Stockport. The Library Street building belatedly gave it a town hall to be proud of, and found an innovative and fitting use for Briggs and Wolstenholme's beautiful college building.

Indeed, it was invariably on the college steps that civic dignitaries posed for photographs with honoured guests. Andrew Carnegie was photographed there in 1909 when he was granted the Freedom of the Borough in 1909 in recognition of his generous donations to erect Pemberton Library, opened 1907, and to the Maypole Disaster Fund in 1908.

Andrew Carnegie's gift of £5,000 in 1902 paid for Pemberton Library, which opened in 1907. He came to Wigan in 1909 to receive the freedom of the Borough.

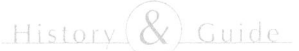

The Maypole Colliery disaster at Abram was the major story in Wigan in 1908. Seventy-five people were killed when gas ignited during shot-firing in the pit on 18 August 1908. Only three men escaped alive. The story was extensively covered in the national as well as the local press, with journalists and photographers from the *Times* taking their place alongside staffers from the *Wigan Observer*. Some of the photographs produced drew strong emotional reaction from those who saw them – families crowding around the pit head hoping for news of their loved one. The mine blazed for days after the explosion, until it was eventually flooded to extinguish the flames. Bodies continued to be brought out of the mine for years, and a memorial to the dead was erected in nearby Abram churchyard. In 1983, to mark the 75th anniversary of the disaster, the monument was restored and rededicated.

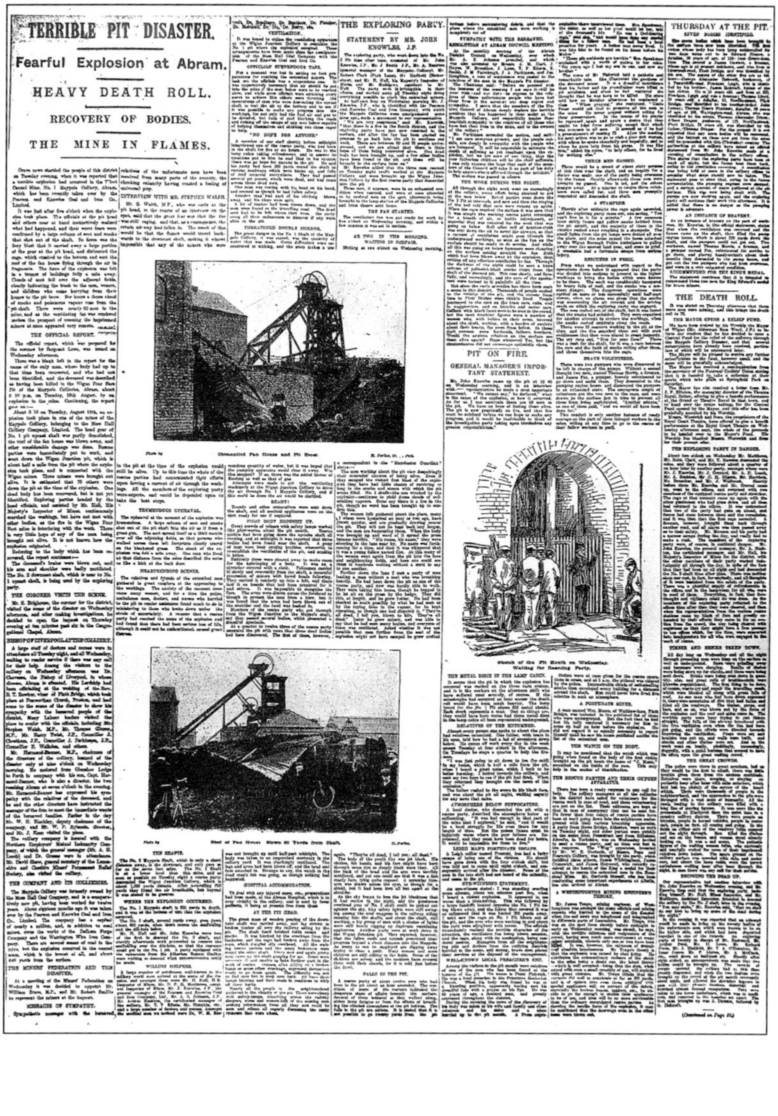

TERRIBLE PIT DISASTER.

Fearful Explosion at Abram.

HEAVY DEATH ROLL.

RECOVERY OF BODIES.

THE MINE IN FLAMES.

THE EXPLORING PARTY.

STATEMENT BY MR. JOHN KNOWLES, J.P.

THURSDAY AT THE PIT.

Dismantled Fan House and Pit Brow.

PIT ON FIRE.

GENERAL MANAGER'S IMPORTANT STATEMENT.

Sketch of the Pit Mouth on Wednesday. Waiting for Rescuing Party.

THE DEATH ROLL.

(Continued on Page 11)

On page 8 of the Wigan Observer, *22 August 1908 – the first of several pages about the disaster – the newspaper made an early use of photography, publishing two photographs by Harry Parkes of Orrell Post.*

On 21 August 1983 – the 75th anniversary of the explosion – the Rector of Wigan, the Rev. Malcolm Forrest, led a moving memorial service in Abram church. Afterwards the restored memorial was rededicated. Here the Mayor of Wigan lays a wreath.

To raise money for the bereaved families, many postcards commemorating the disaster were sold, and one of them actually listed seventy-seven men rather than the true death toll of seventy-five. Two men's tallies were unaccounted for – when they were not down the mine their tallies should have been on a tally-board in the lamp room – and the men were assumed to have died. Both men had actually lost their tallies, and failed to report the fact!

At the inquest which followed, everyone blamed everyone else for the accident, and local mine owners swore in court that there was no gas in Wigan pits – something every miner knew to be untrue. The jury endorsed a long list of recommendations for making mining a safer occupation, but the loss of over 300 lives in what was almost a carbon-copy explosion at nearby Westhoughton only four years later suggests few of them had been implemented!

Despite the ever-present horror of mining disasters, Wiganers knew how to celebrate – and happily lined the streets in huge numbers for civic processions, carnivals, Royal visits, and their annual 'Walking Days'.

A popular religious event for just about every church in the town was the annual 'Walking Day' – here Standishgate is lined with people for St Mary's Walking Day in 1915.

Wigan 'Northern Union' (Rugby League) star Jimmy Leytham retired in 1912 having scored 312 tries – then a world record.

King George V and Queen Mary visited the town in July 1913, and were received by the Mayor of Wigan on a specially constructed dais in the Market Square. This was part of a Royal Tour of the North of England, and the Royal party drove around the town along streets lined with their loyal subjects. A year later many of those who had welcomed the king were answering his call to arms and preparing for war.

Wigan men were in action almost from the outbreak of war – at Mons, a coal-mining town just like home! Throughout November and December 1914, They saw action in both cavalry and infantry regiments – both of which suffered significant losses. Those early actions prompted one Wigan soldier to write home with the sombre message that those who believed the war would be over by Christmas were sadly mistaken.

The early months of 1915 saw a number of local men enduring the horrors of Ypres, trapped in a wedge of low-lying land amidst the ruins of the town and surrounded by Germans. The conditions were appalling – abetted by the fact that it was a very wet spring, and by the end of May, the men were living and fighting in trenches deep in water.

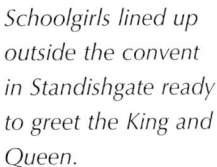

Schoolgirls lined up outside the convent in Standishgate ready to greet the King and Queen.

King George V steps down from the dais erected in front of the Market Hall in the Market Square on 10 July 1913 after being welcomed to Wigan by the mayor, Alderman Dickinson.

The town had buried its first casualty of the war as early as November 1914, and on the same day, many local men attended a recruitment rally in the Pavilion Theatre, and signed up to go to France and Belgium.

And so it continued for years, and for some of those soldiers who survived, 1917 found them back in the area of Ypres. Although many of them must have felt as though they had never left the mud of Flanders area, the battles they would engage in at what became known as Passchendaele would leave them mentally scarred for life.

Wigan sent a second Territorial Army unit to Flanders in early 1917 – the 2/5th Manchester Regiment, part of the 66th Division, and in October 1917 they were in the thick of the fighting in the battles leading up to and including Passchendaele. Many of them never returned home.

At home people busied themselves with fund-raising work to help the war effort, and towards the end of the conflict, a tank was displayed just inside the gates of Mesnes Park to encourage further 'giving'. It remained there, rusting away, until 1935.

The horror of the war touched the town considerably as the death toll grew longer, and as letters from the troops at the front described conditions many would have believed to be impossible. It hit it directly, however, in April 1918, when a Zeppelin dropped bombs hoping to damage the Wigan Coal & Iron Company's Kirkless Iron Works. They missed, but hit properties in New Springs, killing five people and injuring nine more.

But as all wars do, the conflict came to an end, and the town honoured its dead with a fine War Memorial executed by the great Sir Giles Gilbert Scott and erected in front of the town's Parish Church. It was unveiled in 1925, some five years after the last soldier had returned home. War memorials were also erected in Platt Pridge, and at Wigan Golf Club, Standish Collieries, and in just about every one of the local neighbourhoods.

Calderbanks staff were photographed demolishing the First World War tank in Mesnes Park in 1935.

The soldiers returned to a very different town to the one they had left. The social order at home had been upturned by the need to keep the country running with so many men away fighting, and in the 1920s, a slightly more egalitarian culture than had existed before 1914 began to emerge. But it was a lot poorer, and many of the advances in living and working conditions which had been won in the years before the war had been lost by the end.

A cotton strike in late 1918 added to local hardships, and the depressed post-war economy added to the problems with reduced demand for the materials produced in Wigan. The first colliery closure in the area was announced in 1920 – Douglas Bank Colliery – and although the town's factories and mills reverted to their pre-war production, few offered full employment, and the town's first cotton mill closures were announced at about the same time. Widespread poverty was reported, and the effects of years of neglect on the town centre housing stock saw once neat and well-kept property become appalling slums. A massive slum-clearance and rebuilding programme followed and continued throughout the 1920s and '30s. But while the insanitary living conditions of the pre-war era were largely swept away, it was at a price. Rents on the new housing were considerably higher than the insanitary hovels they replaced.

While conducting research for his book *The Road to Wigan Pier*, Eric Blair, better known as George Orwell, visited the town in 1937, and found that despite the house-building programme, the town still had major problems. He wrote:

> Ever since the war, in the complete impossibility of getting houses, parts of the population have overflowed into supposed temporary quarters in fixed caravans. Wigan, for instance, with a population of 85,000 has round about 200 caravan dwellings with a family in each – perhaps somewhat near 1,000 people in all ground on which the caravans have been dumped like rubbish shot out of a bucket. The majority are old single decker buses (the rather smaller buses of ten years ago) which have been taken off their wheels and propped up with struts of wood. The dirt and congestion of these places is such that you cannot well imagine it unless you have tested it with your own eyes and more particularly your nose. It is almost impossible to sleep on the floor, because the damp soaks up from below. I was shown mattresses which were still wringing wet at eleven in the morning.

The start of the local trade holidays had been seen in the town in 1917, despite the demands of war production, and in 1919 the annual Wigan Week holiday was instigated. For decades thereafter the town virtually shut down for an annual holiday week each July or August. The post-war era also saw the reinstatements of many of the local entertainments which had been suspended during the war, and slowly life returned to normal.

The driver stands proudly in front of a new Model T van painted in the livery of J. Gregory & Sons, grocers and bakers of Ince in the 1920s.

Getting around the town improved in the post-war era – Wigan bought its first buses in 1919 – those same ones which Orwell wrote about years later – and the Corporation experimented briefly with trolley buses in the late 1920s. By the early 1930s, however, all four of the trolley buses, and many of the trams had been replaced by buses. Before that, the town had introduced the beginnings of its one-way traffic system. King Street became one way as early as 1927, and 'robot policemen' (traffic lights to us) first appeared in the town at the junction of Standishgate and Mesnes Street in 1930. Pedestrian crossings – the first of thirty-six – complete with Belisha beacons first appeared five years later.

The 1920s also saw the first local MP become a member of the government: Stephen Walsh, MP for Ince, became minister of War in the January 1924 Liberal/Labour Coalition Government, but his cabinet career was cut short when the Torys were returned to power only nine months later!

Hardship in the town was exacerbated by the miners' strike in 1926, and the National Strike which grew out of it. That hardship and poverty placed a huge burden on the Wigan Poor Law Union and the local churches who tried to feed the hungry with soup kitchens, but they could do nothing about the disease that accompanied it. Smallpox was recorded in the town in 1927, and again ten years later, and tuberculosis was almost endemic. The Wrightington Tuberculosis Hospital opened in 1933, and was kept very busy!

In that same year many Wiganers joined a hunger march to London, and another which started from the town in 1934. By 1936, there were over 12,000 people on the dole – representing unemployment in the town of over 30 per cent – and almost two thirds of that number had been unemployed since the late 1920s!

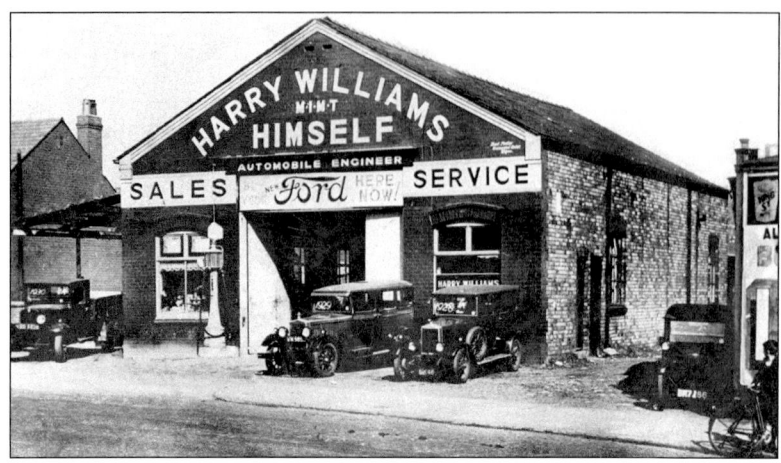

Harry Williams' Garage in Mesnes Road in the 1930s – with a single petrol pump on the forecourt and a selection of secondhand cars from the late 1920s.

Many more factories, collieries and mills had closed by 1936, and in that year the last of the blast furnaces at the huge Kirkless plant were demolished.

As a sign of the times, Wigan's police force fitted some of their cars with radios in 1933, and in that same year the celebrated star Gracie Fields visited the town on 16 September, to start 'motor car reliability trials' from the Market Square.

In 1936 major news stories included the opening of the new Bus Station on the Market Square – built at a cost of £6,000, and the Harp Inn in Scholes being struck by lightening! In the following year, the huge Ritz Cinema in Station Road opened its doors for the first time. Now it has finally closed – leaving no cinemas in the town centre – and plans are afoot to replace it and much of the surrounding land with another huge shopping centre.

September 1938 saw the ominous delivery to the town of civilian gas masks, preparing the town for the inevitable war. A year later, the colours

The Prince of Wales, later King Edward VIII, boards the Royal Train at North Western Station in 1932, four years before he became King.

A group of workers in the machine shop at Park Forge in the 1930s.

The Mayor and Aldermen take the salute during a 1941 Warship Week parade in the Market Square.

of the TA unit were handed to the Mayor for safe-keeping, and the town's cinemas, theatres and sports venues were closed for the duration. Church bells were silenced on 31 December 1939 – the first time since the end of the Great War – and a steady stream of Wiganers appeared in court for breaking the blackout – one simply for lighting a cigarette!

World War II came to Wigan in an unusual way – on 1 September 1939 the first of over 600 people were evacuated to the 'safety' of Wigan from Manchester and Salford. The next day an air raid siren test caused some panic, as few people had been forewarned of it, and by the end of the month, the war had claimed Wigan's first fatality – Ezekiel Livesay from Wallgate, a serving member of the Royal Navy. Another unannounced air raid test in November caused widespread panic in the town, but from December all subsequent tests were well advertised in advance!

The local paper, the *Wigan Observer*, reported in early November that a Wigan mother and her children had been lost a few days earlier on board a liner sunk in the Atlantic by a German U-Boat, but for most people, the early days of the war were punctuated by exhortations to dig for victory – turning gardens and allotments over to intensive vegetable growing! The food problems encountered during the First World War had been quickly forgotten, and by the outbreak of World War II, Britain was importing more than 70 per cent of its food! Several times throughout the war, the paper repeated the need to plant and grow more food.

The town was involved in several fundraising campaigns – a Spitfire Appeal in 1940, War Weapons Week in December 1940, a Warship Week in 1941, and several special fundraisers supported by Wigan's Mayors.

Her Majesty the Queen steps off the Royal train at Wigan North Western Station.

John Lennon on stage in Manchester in 1965. Two years earlier, on 13 October 1963, the Beatles played two shows at the ABC Wigan.

Despite the intensive bombing of Manchester and Liverpool, Wigan survived the conflict virtually unscathed. The town was bombed once, but the intended target – Pagefield Iron Works – was undamaged.

Shortly before the end of the war, the King and Queen made their second visit to Wigan on 7 March 1945, and visited Pagefield Iron Works – they had previously visited on 20 May 1938 when they had been welcomed by the Mayor on a dais built against the Market Hall with the same ceremony which had welcomed his father King George V a quarter of a century earlier.

Our present Queen made the first of her three visits so far to the town in the early 1950s. She visited again as part of her Silver Jubilee tour in 1977, and to open Wigan Pier in 1986.

Post-war Wigan embarked on a period of extensive redevelopment, with a rapid expansion in the building of new houses, and extensive industrial regeneration.

Lord Crawford decided to move his family to Scotland – back to Balcarres in Fife, the family's ancestral home – and offered Haigh Hall and the Plantations to the County Borough Council for a token sum of £18,000 in 1947. That generous offer led to the establishment of the Haigh Hall Country Park we enjoy today.

Just as the Edwardian era had been the era of the music hall in Wigan, so the 1930s, 40s and 50s were undoubtedly the era of the cinema. In the years immediately following the war, there were seven cinemas in the town centre – the County Playhouse, the Court, the Empire, the Palace, the Pavilion, Prince's, and the Ritz, with two more in Scholes – the Picture House and the Labour Hall – two in Pemberton, and the little Gidlow Picture House in Gidlow Lane, now a kitchen and fitted wardrobe manufacturer's. But the advent of television in the 1950s sounded the death-knell of cinemas throughout the country. Today there are no cinemas in the centre at all – the great Ritz where Buddy Holly played in March 1958 and the Beatles in October 1963 stands empty – it was billed as the 'Ritz Theatre' in 1958, but the 'ABC Wigan' by 1963. The Court, Prince's and the Playhouse are now all clubs and bars. EMI closed the ABC in the early 1980s, but it was revived and reopened by Peter Hannavy a few years later. The economics of a town-centre cinema could not compete with the Virgin Megaplex at Robin Park, and it closed again a few years later.

For other theatres and cinemas, fate was not so kind. The Hippodrome burned to the ground in the early 1950s, and the Pavilion – which had at various times housed a circus venue and a skating rink and well as a dance hall – was demolished in 1959 to make way for the Wigan International Pool. Prince's Cinema barely survived the 1960s, closing in 1970, screening *Jack the Ripper* as its last film, while the Court – originally the Royal Court Theatre – showed its last film a few years later in 1973.

Heinz had originally set up their operation in the former munitions factory at Bradley Hall in Standish after the war before moving to their huge new manufacturing base in Kitt Green in 1959.

On the industrial front, the changes which befell post-war Wigan were enormous. One by one the mines closed, and one by one the mills closed. Considering the huge numbers of people who were put out of work by these closures, the success of the local authority in attracting new businesses into the town was crucial.

For many years after the town ceased to be a major mining community, the many manufacturing concerns which supported the coal industry continued to thrive until they eventually lost out to overseas suppliers. By the 1970s, Wigan's manufacturing base had moved from being dependent upon two products to hundreds.

Significant amongst the newcomers was Heinz, whose vast plant at Kitt Green once employed well over 3,000 people. While now employing rather fewer, it is a still a major employer in the town.

Wigan's last weaving shed, photographed in 1987 just before it closed. This shed was part of the Dorma factory which occupied a small part of the huge Eckersleys Mill complex near the canal.

Even for the early 1980s, this image shows an unusually quiet moment on the M6 from the Junction 27 bridge at Standish.

Companies like Heinz, Great Universal Stores, JJB Sports and many others settled, expanded and thrived in the town largely because of one thing – the M6. As the railways were replaced by the motorways, towns like Wigan with good motorway access suddenly became very attractive to those companies for whose operations consisted largely of distribution.

The changes the M6 has brought to the town have been considerable – today thousands of jobs depend on the close proximity of the road. But the building of the motorway foreshadowed the enormous growth in car ownership which has strangled the town. Despite the best efforts of the planners, Wigan's one-way system is a nightmare. Forty years ago, street parking coped with the needs of visiting car drivers. The now-demolished Millgate Multi-Storey Car Park built in the 1960s – perhaps a little before its time – remained less than half full most days until well into the 1970s. Today the town is short of parking spaces, and the ring road which once solved the town's traffic chaos is now frequently bottlenecked.

Wigan's skyline in 1970 – St James's Church, Poolstock, seen from the top floor of Wigan's first multi-storey car park on the corner of Millgate and Station Road.

The town's first shopping mall – the ill-considered Wigan Centre Arcade built in the 1970s – swept away some delightful old buildings, courtyards and alleyways, as well as at least a couple of much loved pubs, the Commercial and the Legs o' Man. It was refurbished in the late 1980s as the Marketgate Shopping Centre, but today stands half empty. The recent opening of the Royal Arcade has resulted in many more empty stores in the Galleries and Standishgate as big chains have moved to the new mall.

Several other much loved pubs have disappeared over the years including the Saracen's Head – under the point at which the Ring Road meets Wigan lane. The Park Hotel formerly stood where the new Market Hall stands today – but at least its interior was dismantled and rebuilt in the 'Way We Were' Heritage Centre at Wigan Pier when the Galleries were built in the 1980s.

The 1970s was a period when the town seemed almost embarrassed about itself – embarrassed by the legacy of George Orwell and of George Formby Senior – and sought to cover its embarrassment with decisions which now seem ill-advised. Commissioning postmarks which read 'Wigan - Hub of the North West' and 'Modern Wigan Has No Peer' rather than playing down the seedier aspects of the town's past, actually perpetuated the joke.

The building of the brutally unattractive concrete slab Civic Centre in Millgate at the same time – so totally out of character with the rest of the town – also smacked of a Borough uncertain about who or what it was, or what it wanted to be. The subsequent building of the Wiend Centre nearby, and the adoption of the old mining College as a fitting Town Hall just makes this building seem all the more out of place as a focal point for civic life in the town. Phase 2 was designed with an open piazza

Scholes flats seen from the open piazza which was originally a feature of Phase 2 of the Civic Centre development. Mercifully, Phase 3 was never built.

which would have eventually looked over the third and final phase of the development – which thankfully was never built. The piazza was filled in within a few years to meet the Council's ever increasing demand for office space and The site earmarked for phase 3 – where the legendary *Wigan Casino* once stood – is now scheduled to become part of the huge new shopping centre planned to straddle today's Station Road.

The Metropolitan Borough of Wigan – the monolith created during local government reorganisation – combined Leigh, Tyldesley, Atherton, Hindley, Standish and a dozen other local communities into one authority and alternative uses were found for a handful of redundant town halls. A few years ago, the title of 'Borough' so proudly used since 1246 was dropped from the Council's paperwork and from the livery on its vehicles. Now simply known as 'Wigan Council', a little bit of heritage has been sidelined.

'The Way We Were' at Wigan Pier, a joke for so long, enjoyed twenty-one years as a thriving tourist attraction, drawing visitors from all over the world, before closing in 2007. A question mark, however, now hangs over it as the plans for the Wigan Pier Quarter emerge.

Central Park, so long the home of Wigan Football Club is now a Tesco supermarket – a bronze rugby ball the only reminder of its past importance in the social and sporting life of the town. Wigan Warriors now play at the new JJB stadium, at Robin Park outside of the town centre, the new focus of social life with its clubs, cinemas and restaurants.

The bronze sculpture of a rugby ball, inscribed with the names of some of Wigan's 'greats' is all that remains of Central Park, the home of Wigan Rugby from 1902.

Wigan Athletic AFC, also based at the JJB, have enjoyed several – sometimes difficult – seasons of Barclays Premiership football, reached the 2006 Carling Cup Final, amd now attract bigger crowds than the Warriors.

But the town centre is slowly dying in the face of competition from out-of-town shopping, and it will take a significant effort by the council to breathe life back into it if Wigan is to have a future as memorable as its past.

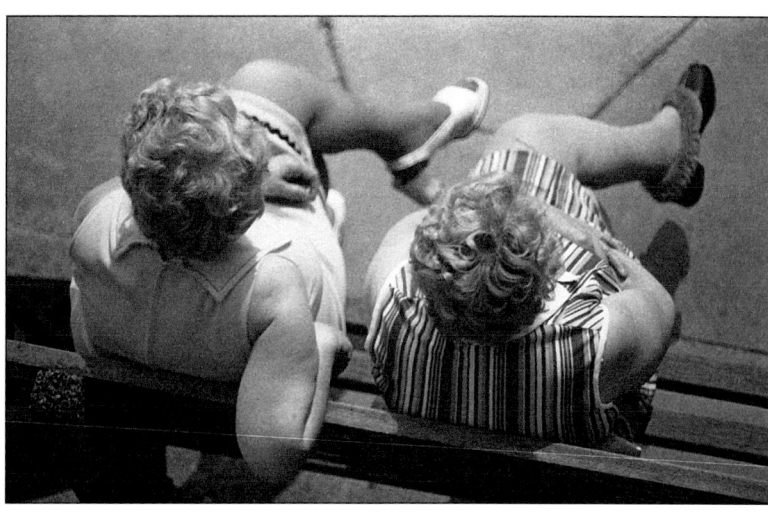

Very 1970s – two women putting the world to rights on a bench in Station Road c.1973.

CHAPTER 9
Famous Wigan, Famous Wiganers

Wigan's fame has spread far and wide, and for a whole range of reasons. Orwell's *Road to Wigan Pier* presented a view of the town in the 1930s which, while not entirely without foundation, was harsher than the reality. But Wigan became, in the minds of many, the archetype of the decaying industrial town where Victorian enterprise – and even enlightenment – had become the run-down squalor that was much of the town at that time. George Formby Senior perpetuated the Wigan Pier joke, and left the town with the overwhelming feeling that it was being laughed at rather than laughed with! And yet, the idea of a pier so far from the sea is a genuinely funny one, and one which the town has since learned to enjoy. Jack Winstanley's lyrics for his song *The Ballad of Wigan Pier* combined the joke with fact – thanks to years of pleasure boating from the tippler now known as Wigan Pier, generations of people did have a lovely day there! Thanks to the enlightened development of the canal basin in the 1980s, the last laugh was undoubtedly enjoyed by the town, who saw their heritage centre opened by Her Majesty the Queen, and pick up a handful of awards.

When Wigan's pit brow lasses posed for dozens of picture postcards in the early years of the twentieth century, they were already famous.

When That Lass o' Lowrie's *was republished in the 1980s, these Wigan pit lasses were featured on the cover.*

Indeed, they had already been written about in the wonderfully difficult-to-read novel *That Lass o' Lowrie's* published in 1877 by the eminent American novelist Frances Hodgson Burnett who is best known for *The Secret Garden* and *Little Lord Fauntleroy*. For an American to write about the Wigan coalfields is one thing; to write her novel in Wigan dialect is quite another. Burnett spelled the words as she heard them – creating words and sentences which are virtually unreadable unless read out loud! 119 years later, in 1996, another eminent writer, Martin Cruz Smith – of *Gorky Park* fame – also tackled the subject, having been enchanted by the pictures of the pit lasses he had seen on show in *The Way We Were* heritage centre during a visit to Wigan. His book *Rose* is an old-fashioned romantic thriller in which, however, he rewrote the geography of Wigan as well as some of the history! But it is full of local surnames and people named after local places – his character *Reverend Maypole* disappears on the day of a terrible mining disaster where seventy-six men died. Neither *Rose* nor *That Lass o' Lowrie's* was particularly successful, but as evidence of enduring interest in Wigan and its people, they are fine examples.

If romantic fiction set in Wigan is not to everyone's taste, it seems that another confection is – Uncle Joe's Mint Balls ('keep you all aglow') are sold throughout the world, and many a person probably knows of the town only through the legend 'Made by Wm. Santus and Co. Ltd., Wigan, England'. The strong peppermint sweets have been made in the town since 1898 using the same traditional – and still secret – recipe used by Mrs Santus when she originally made the sweets in her kitchen in 1898. As the company's website proudly proclaims 'despite the fact that Uncle Joe's Mint Balls are made only in Wigan, their fame has spread far and wide. Uncle Joe's have been sighted at the top of mountains in India, villages in Kenya, Vancouver in Canada and even in the darkest depths of New York, USA!'

For those with memories long enough, bands like *Wigan's Chosen Few* and *Wigan's Ovation* briefly carried the town's name into the pop scene. And then, of course, from the 1980s there was Limahl from Kajagoogoo!

To aficionados of Northern Soul, however, Wigan is best remembered thanks to the famous Wigan Casino, demolished twenty-four years ago, in 1984, but still renowned for its 'all-nighters' which brought thousands of fans from far and wide in the 1970s and into the very early 1980s. It had been built in 1912 as the eminently respectable *Empress Ballroom*, it became the Casino in the mid-1960s, and its original owners can never have anticipated its future fame! When the all-nighters started, there was a modicum of indignant outrage from some quarters within the town at the hoards of the 'great unwashed' who spilled out of the Casino on to the streets in the early hours of Sunday mornings, but over the years the fame of the venue earned it a sort of respectability. It spawned a number

One of the most instantly recognisable products to come out of Wigan is the famous red tin containing Uncle Joe's Mint Balls – now sold throughout the world.

The magnificent Empire Ballroom, built in 1912 which entered rock history as Wigan Casino, scene of the legendary 'all-nighters' in the 1970s.

of career revivals amongst American soul singers, made the careers of several disc-jockeys, was the subject of several series on BBC radio, and even launched a record label.

More recently, the worldwide fame of *The Verve* who started performing together while at Winstanley College, put the town back in the music spotlight once again.

The town also claims several famous sons and daughters, and although their Wigan roots may never have been widely publicised, many stars of radio, television and cinema have strong links with Wigan. Colin Bean, who still lives in Wigan, is best known as Private Sponge in the long-running television series *Dad's Army*. Charlie Olden, better known as Ted Ray, the music hall, film and radio comedian, whose BBC Light Programme series *Ray's a Laugh* ran from the late 1940s to the early 1960s, was born in the Wigan in 1905, the year after the town's most famous son, George Formby OBE. The fine comic actor Roy Kinnear – who first shot to fame in the television series *That Was the Week That Was* and the Beatles' first film *A Hard Day's Night* was born in 1934 in Mesnes Road. Sir Ian McKellen attended Wigan Grammar School, and lived for a time in Parsons Walk, while Ashton-born Joe Gormley, onetime tenacious leader of the National Union of Mineworkers lived for many years in Shevington.

The town was also the home of two famous painters – both of them contemporaries of Lowry. Theodore Major, a fine 'primitive' painter, was born in Wigan in 1908, and the eccentric James Lawrence Isherwood in 1917. Major spent much of his life between two houses in Appley Lane, Appley Bridge – he lived in one and worked in the other – while Isherwood lived and worked at 151 Wigan Lane. Their work is now much in demand. All these people, and many more, have helped make Wigan famous.

History & Guide

Walking Tour 1: Wigan Town Centre

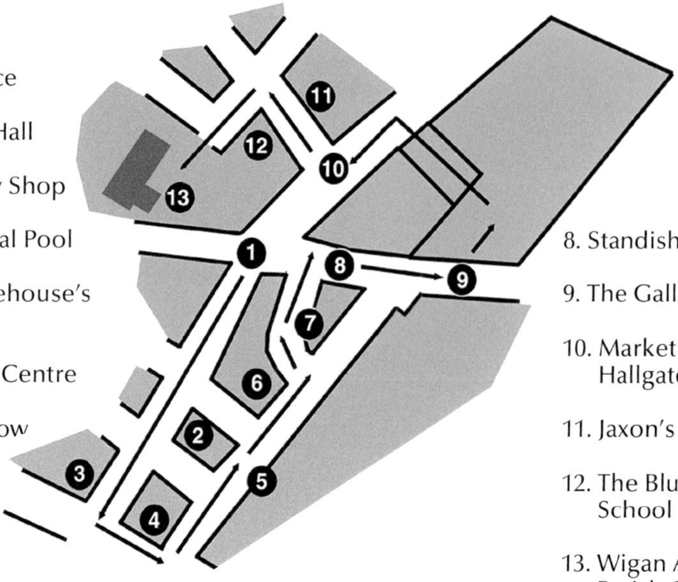

1. Market Place
2. The Town Hall
3. The History Shop
4. International Pool
5. Thos. Whitehouse's House
6. The Wiend Centre
7. Cooper's Row
8. Standishgate
9. The Galleries
10. Market St & Hallgate
11. Jaxon's Court
12. The Bluecoat School
13. Wigan All Saints Parish Church

Walking Tour 2: Wigan Pier

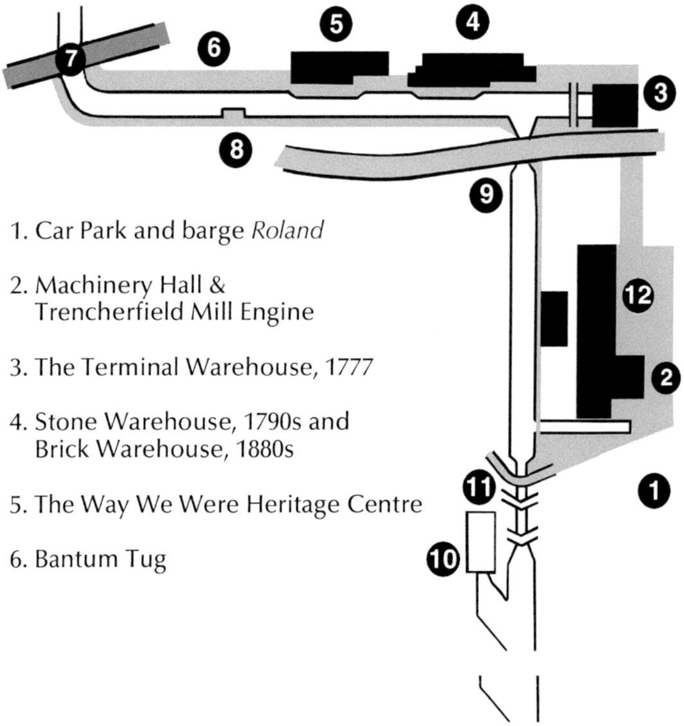

1. Car Park and barge *Roland*
2. Machinery Hall & Trencherfield Mill Engine
3. The Terminal Warehouse, 1777
4. Stone Warehouse, 1790s and Brick Warehouse, 1880s
5. The Way We Were Heritage Centre
6. Bantum Tug
7. Seven Stars Bridge
8. Wigan Pier
9. Crossover bridge
10. Dry Dock
11. Bottom Lock
12. Opie's Museum of Memories

Walking Tour 1: Wigan Town Centre

This walk starts in the Market Place, the historic centre of Wigan since medieval times, and now the site of the pavement sculpture installed to commemorate the 750th anniversary of the first royal charter of 1246 which granted 'that the lands at Wygayun may be a borough for ever, and that the burgesses of the same borough may have a Guild merchant, with a treasury and other liberties and free customs'.

The Market Place in the closing months of the twentieth century, with the new centrepiece installed to commemorate the 750th anniversary of the granting of the town's first royal charter. A century earlier, the left of this view was occupied by a small hut and a water hydrant servicing the town's steam-powered tramcars (see colour page 1).

Walking Tour

The site of the entrance to today's Marketgate Shopping Centre, as it looked in the 1890s. At that time, the street lamps were in the centre of the roadway – another one was sited further down towards the top of Standishgate – and apart from the newly introduced steam trams, horse-drawn traffic was the order of the day.

Markets were held here for centuries – farmers and merchants brought their merchandise in to the centre of the town to be sold at stalls which ran right round the Market Place, and part way down Standishgate. The market moved further west with the establishment of the Market Square and, later, with the building of the Market Hall in 1877.

As you stand facing the Parish Church, the site now occupied by Barclays Bank was, until the mid-1980s, Lowe's Victoria House department store, established by James Lowe in 1887. It closed in 1985, and when the site was cleared, the parish church was revealed in all its glory from Market Place. Sadly, commercial considerations meant the site could not be kept clear, and the present bank buildings were erected, taking over the sites of two pubs as well. Had that development been under consideration today, nearly more than two decades later, the planning decision might have been very different.

The top of Market Street – formerly part of Hallgate – viewed from Market Place, c.1902. Electric trams had been newly introduced, and the street was undergoing a lot of rebuilding. The hoardings on the right are on the site now occupied by Thomas Cook's travel agency.

Walking Tour

Market Place, looking towards Standishgate – the alleyway in the centre of the picture is Cooper's Row, one of the only two surviving medieval lanes in this part of town.

The section of Market Street which runs down past the banks was, in olden times, part of medieval Hallgate, following a zig-zag route to the rectory, known as Wigan Hall.

Hallgate was one of the main four mediaeval streets or 'gata' – the others being Millgate, Standishgate and Wallgate (which may originally have been Wellgate), their names reminding us of the Norse period in the town's history. The origins of two other streets with the 'gate' suffix, Bishopgate and Stairgate, is unknown, but, of course, none of the above implies gates in a walled town. The Norse word for 'gate' was 'bar', as in Micklegate Bar in York. There is a seventh 'gate' – Bradshawgate – in Scholes about half a mile away on the other side of the River Douglas, an interesting reminder that Scholes was the site of the original Norse settlement in the tenth century.

> **From the Market Place walk towards the top of Wallgate and turn left into Library Street. Walk down Library Street to the Town Hall.**

Library Street was created in the 1870s, a new opening being created from Market Place. Before then, a jumble of narrow lanes and yards had occupied the whole of the east side of Market Place, of which only traces remain. Wholesale clearance of those properties gave the opportunity to establish the street plan as we see it today.

Towards the bottom of Library Street, the building which now houses Wigan's Town Hall was one of the first important construction projects in the town in the twentieth century. It was originally built as Wigan

Walking Tour

From near Waterhouse's 1877 Library at the bottom of the street, this view was taken shortly after the Technical College building was completed in 1903. An extension was added at the back in the 1920s. The Pavilion Theatre and Wigan Hippodrome were built on the empty plot to the right in 1909. The International Pool now occupies the site.

The seventeenth-century town seal realised in terracotta, above the main doorway of the Town Hall in Library Street.

and District Mining and Technical College, with the top floor specially designed as the first permanent home for the town's School of Art. The north facing roof lights of the art school's drawing studios can still be seen by looking up at the Hewlett Street side of the building.

Wigan was rightly proud of its somewhat enlightened education system in the second half of the nineteenth century. The college had been founded in the 1880s, housed in a strange metal-sided building on the site of the present swimming pool, and was already fifteen years old when the new building was opened. Long before that however – in 1857 – the town's first Mining School had been established, only the second such establishment in Britain. Art classes can also be traced back to the 1850s, making the town's art school one of the first in the country. The new college was lavishly equipped for its day, with workshops and studios, and apparently even had its own mine shaft! When the college moved out – to premises at Rylands Mill near Mesnes Park and to Trencherfield Mill at Wigan Pier – this magnificent building became the Town Hall.

Built between 1901 and 1903 and designed by Briggs and Wolstenholme, the building is faced with glazed red terracotta bricks, and fronted with an impressive entrance supported by terracotta pillars. Above the doorway, a three-dimensional interpretation of the town's seventeenth-century seal can be seen. Surprisingly, the borough did not have a coat of arms until the late 1920s, so this seal was widely used.

Further down Library Street, on the corner with Rodney Street, is Alfred Waterhouse's Library and Reading Room, built in the neo-Gothic style in 1877 and opened in 1878. When the lending library moved into the basement of the new Town Hall, the public library and reading room was converted into the innovative History Shop, with a splendid exhibition about life in the town. It is well worth a visit.

Walking Tour

The Reference Library occupies the top floor of Waterhouse's Gothic building on the corner of Library Street and Rodney Street.

> **At the foot of Library Street, turn left past Wigan International Pool, and left again into Millgate and up the hill.**

Turn left at the foot of Library Street across the front of the International Pool, built in the 1960s on the site of the Pavilion and Hippodrome theatres.

In its day, the building of the pool was a major civic achievement, as Wigan became only the fifth town in Britain to build an Olympic-size pool. Built over former mine workings, it turned out to be a challenging construction project.

Turn left again up the side of the pool into Millgate, which used to continue down the hill to the River Douglas, but the creation of the ring road in the 1980s cut a swathe through it.

Half way up, on the right is the fine late Georgian house, now used as a furniture warehouse, which was the home of eighteenth-century liquor merchant, local historian and amateur artist Thomas Whitehouse.

The Wigan Heritage Service has a fine manuscript history of the town written by Whitehouse, and illustrated with his charming primitive pen and wash drawings.

> **Opposite the Civic Centre, turn left into the Wiend.**

Further up Millgate, the Wiend Centre is built on the site of first- and second-century buildings, contemporary with the Roman settlement

Walking Tour

Until very recently, Thomas Whitehouse's fine five-bay late-Georgian house in Millgate has been used as a discount furniture warehouse.

The Wiend Centre was built on the side of Ezra Sidebottom's printing works. While the site was clear, Greater Manchester Archaeological Unit 's excavations confirmed that the site had been occupied by large wooden buildings in the first and second centuries, the period of the Roman settlement of Coccium.

of *Coccium*. The Wiend itself has existed since mediaeval times, but this area was only opened up after the demolition of a closely grouped assortment of buildings in the late 1970s and 1980s. Another small alleyway, Cooper's Row, gave access in Victorian times to the Old Dog Concert Room Hall, and later to the Alexandra Hall, the first purpose-built music hall in the town.

When the site was cleared, only the house next to the Wiend Centre, and the nearby John Bull Chop House in Coopers Row were spared, together with the eighteenth-century buildings fronting on to the upper section of the Wiend itself.

Walking Tour

A century ago Coopers Row led to the Old Dog Music Concert Rooms, and the Alexandra Music Hall – the success of the latter brought about the demise of the former. The last of the ancient buildings along this alleyway survives today as the John Bull Chop House.

Walk down the Wiend and return to the Market Place. Turn right and walk to the top of Standishgate.

As you return to Market Place, take a few minutes to look at the buildings. The mock-Tudor buildings, many of them constructed during the second half of the nineteenth century, define the character of today's Wigan. Most subsequent rebuildings in the town centre have continued to echo that character, despite the fact that Wigan had relatively few original sixteenth- or seventeenth-century black and white timbered buildings.

The Marketgate Shopping Centre, the entrance of which faces you, was built in the 1970s as the Wigan Centre, and was built to a brutally stark design. It replaced a number of small alleyways and yards, and an old arcade which ran down towards the original market hall. There were three Victorian arcades in the town centre, two of which still survive.

The finest of them, Makinson Arcade, is on the left as you walk down Standishgate. It was opened in 1898, designed by Robert Ablett, and its fine entrance is one of the few noteworthy architectural features surviving on today's Standishgate. The arcade itself has had so many facelifts that few original features survive. Once the busiest traffic street in Wigan, the pedestrianised Market Place and Standishgate do, however, create a pleasant open space.

Walking Tour

Staff pose for the camera outside Marks & Spencer's store in the Makinson Arcade in 1925. The policy of charging a penny for every item in Michael Marks' original penny bazaar was to conceal the fact that with his poor English, he found discussing prices with his customers less than easy!

Makinson Arcade has a special place in British retailing history for it was half way down the arcade on the right that Mr Marks and Mr Spencer opened their first shop. Before that, they had operated stalls in Wigan Market Hall, where Michael Marks had traded for several years. Success brought the need for larger premises, and they moved to a larger unit in the Makinson Arcade in 1899. That shop continued in use until 1931 when the company's present store in Standishgate was build.

Continuing down Standishgate, the frontage of the NatWest bank building is worthy of a few moments – built in 1875 and showing influences, according to Pevsner, of eighteenth-century French styling.

Further down on the same side, the huge entrance to the Galleries Shopping Centre echoes the mock Tudor elsewhere in the town centre, but inside the design is that same late twentieth-century hotchpotch which has been imposed on so many modern shopping centres.

> **Turn left into the Galleries Shopping Centre and, keeping to the lower walkway to the right, walk through to Atherton Square.**

Coming out into a small square in the centre of the shopping complex, turn left and continue into Market Street.

Market Street was an important shopping street until the development of the Wigan Centre shopping precinct in the 1970s replaced many of the shops with the goods delivery ramp onto the upper level.

The creation of the Galleries precinct in the 1980s further marred the street, again with a goods entrance, and the backs of many of the stores within the shopping centre. In recent times, the street has been partly pedestrianised, but the town centre has, in effect, moved away from it and relegated it to something of a backwater.

Walking Tour

After leaving the Galleries, turn left into Market Street.

On the opposite side of Market Street from the Galleries, the Queen's Hall Methodist Mission is by far the most imposing building. The site was previously occupied by the wooden photographic studio of one of the town's leading Victorian professional photographers, James Millard, who also had studios in Scholes for a time. Millard, who worked as a photographer from the 1860s until his death, built the old wooden studio himself, and the building is remembered thanks to a single photograph taken by his son.

What a difference a century can make. Just about 100 years separate these views of Market Street seen from the Market Square end of the street. The upper picture, from 1999, is dominated by the access ramp for the Marketgate Shopping Centre, with the Galleries Shopping Centre beyond while, in the Victorian view, c.1900, a row of traditional shops leads down to the old Market Hall.

Walking Tour

Jaxon's Court, a small modern shopping centre, echoes the narrow lanes and yards of old Wigan.

> **Walk up Market Street to the Crofters Arms, and turn right into Hallgate.**

Hallgate originally led from Market Place to Wigan Hall, the home of the Rector of Wigan, who was also Lord of the Manor in mediaeval times. As such it was a very important street indeed. Today it has lost much of its character, but small shopping areas like Jaxons Court come as a pleasing surprise. When Hallgate was laid out, it was either laid around the perimeters of existing buildings, or important lands, for it turns at ninety degrees as it makes its way towards Wigan Hall. Had this been virgin lands, it might have been expected to take a more direct route.

> **Before Hallgate turns right past the bus station and towards the Rectory, turn left into Bishopgate.**

The Coach and Horses, Hallgate, a survival from medieval times, was demolished in the early 1880s just after this picture was taken.

Walking Tour

Turning left into Bishopgate, All Saints Parish Church is straight ahead, and reached through a small arched gateway.

Before reaching the church, however, the small building on the left is Wigan's original Bluecoat School, built in 1773, but looking rather earlier thanks to its intimate proportions and mullioned windows. In this little one-room school, generations of local children were taught.

Church Gardens, the open area between the roadway and the church itself, is fronted by the former Crown Courts and the Magistrates Court. A splendid new building for the courts was opened in Darlington Street adjacent to the main police station in the 1990s.

> **Access to the parish church is through the archway by the side of the Bluecoat School.**

There has been a church on this site since the eleventh century, although the oldest part of the fabric of today's building is 200 years younger.

The evidence for that earlier church is based on the entry in the Domesday Book where land is mentioned as belonging to the church of the Manor of Newton. Today's Wigan was in the manor of Newton, and that mention is taken as being a reference to the earlier church to stand on this hilltop site.

Much of what can be seen from the outside is Victorian – the result of one of many rebuildings which the church has undergone over the years – but the lower courses of the town are original thirteenth century.

The infant class in the Bluecoat School, Hallgate, around 1915. The original school had been established in 1773, and the infant school was added in 1825.

The Bluecoat School, Bishopgate.

Walking Tour

Wigan's All Saints Parish Church, viewed from Bishopgate. A church has stood on this site at least since the middle of the eleventh century, and perhaps even longer.

At the time of the building of the early tower, Wigan church was the only church covering a huge area within the Diocese of Lichfield. Before the time of the Normans, it was part of the Diocese of York, but of any church which might have stood in the town at that time, no trace has been found.

Today's church date's almost entirely from the mid-nineteenth century, but unusually for a Victorian rebuild, is a largely faithful reconstruction of the late-fourteenth- to early-fifteenth-century church that it replaced.

It might not have been thus – plans were afoot for a completely new church, but a rebellion amongst the parishioners was only quelled when a faithful recreation of the original was agreed. The parishioners had been told that the church was in danger of collapse, but with the walls no more than fifteen inches out of vertical, restoration would probably have been possible. Lords Lindsay, however, was keen to build the town a new church, and just about everything except the tower was dismantled.

Walking Tour

The fifteenth-century font from the parish church was rescued from the garden of the rectory in the 1950s, where it had been used for many years to collect rain water!

So total was the reconstruction that Pevsner, in the South Lancashire volume of his *Buildings of England*, describes the church as being the work of Paley and Sharpe, two well-known church builders, before acknowledging that fragments of the earlier building still survive.

We can see something of what the medieval church looked like from an early pen drawing, which shows the upper section of the tower before the present parapet was added. Around the drawing is written 'Wigan Church as it appeared when the east end was destroyed which gave rise to the vulgar saying that they had set the steeple at the wrong end and two compartments were added to the east end by the Bradshaigh family, but it originally extended further eastwards.' This drawing may show the church as it looked in the late fourteenth or early fifteenth century, before a previous major reconstruction.

The Bradshaigh Tomb as it originally looked, the carved figures lying on top of a carved faux sarcophagus.

Walking Tour

The position of the tower is an unusual feature of the building as well as being the most recognisable shape on the town's skyline, and it has recently undergone a major restoration which had it encased in scaffolding for many months.

Very few churches had the tower positioned to the north of the choir, but drawings made before the nineteenth century reconstruction confirm that the relationship between the tower and the church has always been as it is today.

When the nineteenth-century rebuilding work was underway, much early masonry was unearthed, but little of it is evident today. Above the lower thirteenth-century stonework, the tower probably dates from the thirteenth century – the exception being the upper level beneath the parapet which houses the clock, and which was a Victorian embellishment.

Inside, nothing of the original fabric of the church is immediately visible, but there are many features worth noting. Set into a window in the tower, a Roman altar discovered during the nineteenth-century rebuilding can be seen. Being a pagan artifact and long considered an inappropriate item to feature inside a Christian church, it spent many years on the outside wall, but was brought to its present position during one of the twentieth-century restorations. A Celtic cross or unknown origin was also discovered, and it too can be seen in the church.

In what is now known as the Crawford Chapel, but has at various times since mediaeval times been known as the Chapel of the Blessed Virgin Mary, St Mary's Chapel, St Mary's Chancel, the Bradshaigh Chapel, the Balcarres Chapel and the Haigh Chancel, lie the tombs of Sir William and Lady Mabel Bradshaigh. Their story is told in chapter 3.

Lady Mabel set up an endowment in 1338 to support the original chapel and pay the costs of maintaining a priest to say mass daily in it. She and her husband were later buried within its walls.

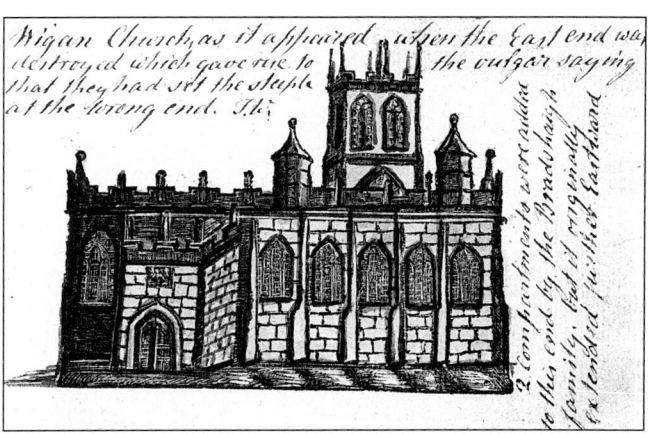

All Saints Church from a pen sketch made before the mid nineteenth-century rebuilding.

Walking Tour

The appearance of their effigies today conceals a traumatic history. The chapel was allowed to fall into ruin after the Reformation in the sixteenth century, and despite several attempts by the Bradshaigh family to restore it, the effigies of Sir William and Lady Mabel were exposed to the increasingly polluted air of Wigan for many years. The damage was considerable, and by the time the present chapel was built, the effigies were in a sorry state. Lady Mabel's effigy was completely restored to cut away the corroded stonework, but Sir William was beyond salvation, and a completely new effigy was created by sculptor John Gibson. The original lies nearby.

They both lay on top of a carved sarcophagus, but it was dismantled many years ago, and the sections of it can be seen lying against the wall. Since then, Sir William and his lady have lain on the floor.

The Walmesley Chapel, off the north aisle, was originally known as the Gerard Chapel, after one of the leading noble families of the area, who once held the lordship of nearby Ince. The chapel probably dates from some time in the fifteenth century, and was the only part of the old church, apart from the tower and the two rood turrets that mark the end of the chancel, not to be rebuilt in the mid-nineteenth century, although subsequent extensive restorations have obscured much of the original masonry.

The chapel was in a very poor state by the mid-seventeenth century, but had been restored before the beginning of the eighteenth. It was completely restored in a second nineteenth-century restoration of the church in the 1890s – so poor had been much of the rebuilding work of 1845-1850, that fifty years later the church was in serious trouble! A further extensive renovation in the 1950s left the chapel – and the rest of the church interior – as it can be seen today.

Outside the south-west door of the church, the open area is dominated by Sir Giles Gilbert Scott's War Memorial, completed in 1925 and unveiled with considerable civic ceremony.

> **From the War Memorial, walk past the Bees Knees pub into Wallgate.**

A number of narrow alleyways used to connect the church with Wallgate and the Market Place, but several have been lost in nineteenth and twentieth-century reconstruction of commercial premises. Three narrow alleyways survive leading to Market Place and Wallgate. Late nineteenth-century photographs confirm that the church has long been hemmed in by buildings, and in one photograph of the lane known as Church Gates, and taken c.1900, the buildings are clearly of no later than late sixteenth-century origin.

The War Memorial, designed by the eminent architect Sir Giles Gilbert Scott, and dedicated in 1925.

Church Gates, c.1900, by John Cooper, one of the town's leading professional photographers. Present day Wigan's love of mock-Tudor buildings, which dates only from the 1920s, is validated by photographs such as this.

Walking Tour

The Bees Knees, formerly the Dog and Partridge, is a surviving example of a Georgian town house. It is seen here through the decorative Victorian canopied railings along the back of one of the buildings which front on to Wallgate.

The area around the war memorial is partly open park, but the south-east side is dominated by the backs of Victorian buildings which front on to upper Wallgate. In recognition of the importance of their location, and despite their rather bland street frontages, the backs of these buildings exhibit some delightful architectural detail, and elaborate Victorian wrought-iron work.

Leaving the war memorial, the Bees Knees public house on the right is one of the few surviving georgian buildings in the centre of Wigan. Beyond it, Wallgate leads down to Wallgate Station, opened by the Lancashire and Yorkshire Railway in 1848, and further down, North Western Station opened twelve years later. Wallgate's frontage dates from an 1896 reconstruction, but the station itself was completely rebuilt in the 1970s. Of the original North Western Station, nothing remains.

Turning left back to the top of Wallgate, look up at the fine frontage of the Raven Hotel on the opposite side of the road.

At the top of Wallgate, we are back in Market Place and at the end of this short tour, finishing up where we started at the commemorative mosaic.

Walking Tour 2: Wigan Pier

No description of Wigan would be complete without an account of Wigan Pier and the restoration of the canal basin which have taken place around it. However the closure of the 'Way We Were' Heritage Centre in December 2007 has left a huge hole in the Wigan Pier Experience. Since this tour was designed in 2003, some parts of the site may not be accessible as the regeneration of what will become the Wigan Pier Quarter continues. If there were no photographs to illustrate the change which has been brought about in the area, it would be hard to imagine just how derelict the area of the town around the Leeds-Liverpool Canal was before the restoration of the 1980s.

Today the pier is signposted from the M6 motorway, and signposts throughout the town direct visitors towards the canal site. Less than three decades ago the town was ashamed of it and seriously considered demolition of those same buildings. In those days the pier itself was just a hump on the towpath, and the canal basin was filled with partially submerged barges.

The starting point is the Trencherfield Mill car park – most main roads into Wigan have signposts to the Pier which will lead to the car park. If on foot, the car park can be reached after a half mile walk down Wallgate from Market Place, past the railway stations, and left through the gates into Trencherfield Mill.

The mill and the outdoor displays dominate the view from the car park. Trencherfield Mill was the last mill to be built alongside the canal in Wigan – all later mills were built near railway lines. While

Perched on a mound at the edge of the car park, Roland was one of the last powered short boats to be built for coal-working on the canal.

History & Guide

Walking Tour

Roland *was acquired as a hulk in the 1980s, and completely rebuilt. This picture was taken shortly after its arrival on site, with Trencherfield Mill behind it.*

The first piece of industrial machinery to arrive on the site in the 1980s was this Glasgow-built steam hammer from 1862.

The mass of the tall mill dominates the static exhibits outside the machinery hall.

Trencherfield had its own canal cutting, later mills had their own sidings. Trencherfield depended entirely on the canal for the delivery of raw materials, and the dispatch of finished products. It also depended on the canal for deliveries of coal to keep the Lancashire boilers fired up.

The preserved barge *Roland*, built in Blackburn in the 1950s, is typical of generations of 'short boats' which plied the canal carrying coal, cotton, and a variety of other goods. *Roland* spend most of its working life as a coal barge, towing a powerless 'butty boat' called *Mary*, and between them they could transport over one hundred tons of coal.

114

Rigby's Patent Steam Hammer was built by Glen and Ross in Glasgow in 1862, and is typical of the machinery found in hundreds of engineering workshops throughout the country – including several in Wigan.

Walking Tour

> *From the car park, walk towards the ticket office and the entrance to the machinery hall.*

Moving towards the entrance to the museum and the ticket office, the edge of the car park is dominated by the huge Walker Bros. Indestructible Ventilating Fan, made at Pagefield Iron Works. These huge rope-driven fans pumped up to a million cubic feet of air a minute into Wigan's mines, and they were used throughout the mining world. Initially designed to be powered by huge stationary steam engines, they provided the constant fresh cool air which effectively made deep mining possible.

The first Trencherfield Mill was built on this site in the early 1820s, with a second mill opening three decades later. The machinery was belt driven, the power being supplied by a central engine house.

The third mill – the remains of which we see today – cost £120,000 to build and was completed for William Woods & Son in 1908. Described as a fireproof spinning mill, it has 60,000 ring spindles and 24,000 mules.

The boiler house, which supplied steam to the great mill engines – of which there were originally three – was on the site in front of today's 'Mill at the Pier' concert and exhibition hall. Next to it, the splendid engine house survives, but a huge free-standing chimney which stood near the engine house at the edge of today's car park was removed during the 1980s development of the site as a tourist attraction. Where the outside machinery is now displayed, in front of the museum entrance, there was originally a large carding room, a single story building with glass roof lights.

A full page report on the mill's opening described how it was up to date in every respect, particular note being made it the canal cutting which had been created to run past the end of the mill and the boiler house.

Only five years after the mill was opened, Woods went in to liquidation, and the site was taken over by Alexander Young and renamed Trencherfield Mill Limited.

Part of the mill was, until recently, still used by a textile company, and the ground floor to the right of the building is Opie's Museum of Memories, to which we will return at the end of this tour. For a few years in the 1980s that accommodation housed the School of Visual Communications and the School of Fashion – the graphic design, photography, video and textile design departments – of the Wigan College of Technology, now known as Wigan and Leigh College.

Walking Tour

Inside the mill, a vast assortment of textile and industrial machinery has been collected together, but the jewel in the crown is undoubtedly the engine room.

When the mill was opened by the Mayor of Wigan, Alderman S. Wood – 'wearing his chain of office,' as reported in the *Wigan Observer* – the wives of local dignitaries were invited to officially name the three steam engines – two of which survive today – and the electric engine. *Rina* and *Helen* were named by Mrs K. Marshall and Mrs O. Rushton respectively, while the third engine was named *Margaret* by Mrs Gaskell. The electric engine – *Jean* – was christened by Mrs Sharrock. The Lady Mayoress then set the engines in motion.

These are four-cylinder triple-expansion engines, with a stroke of 5ft, and nominally rated at 2,100 horse power, using steam pressure of 200lb. For the technically mined, they each have a 25in high pressure cylinder, a 40in intermediate cylinder, and two 44in low pressure cylinders.

Drive is transferred to the huge 26ft-diameter rope drum (actually referred to in the newspaper account as a 26in diameter!) grooved to take the 54 ropes which transferred the power to every floor of the mill.

The interior of the engine house at Trencherfield Mill – and what is believed to be the world's largest working steam engine. The engine is operated regularly, and the town – after years of silence – has once again become used to the regular sound of its whistle.

Walking Tour

That the mill engine is still functioning today is largely due to one man – Ted Melling – who was the engineer in charge of the machinery when the mill closed. He was determined not to let the magnificent engine deteriorate after the mill ceased production, and kept it regularly turned over for several years. Eventually, the world caught up with Melling's vision, and the great engineer was saved and restored to the splendid condition it is in today.

In its heyday, the mill employed over 1,000 people, and contemporary accounts talk of the clatter of clogs on the cobbles as the workers made their way down Wallgate to Trencherfield and the several other mills which dominated the area.

> Turn left after leaving the machinery hall, and leave the Trencherfield Mill site by the gates onto Pottey Road. Cross the road and walk down to the canal side.

The first building, on the right by the canal, enjoys the address 'No.1 Wigan Pier' and was built in 1777 at what was then the terminus of the Liverpool to Wigan canal. The remainder of the canal to Leeds was not completed until 1816.

The Terminal Warehouse was built to a novel design and was one of the first to offer completely enclosed facilities for loading and unloading barges. As the owners were millers, keeping the grain dry as it was unloaded from the barges was essential. Later it was used for a wide variety of cargo traffic, and before it finally went out of use, was partially operated by a company importing tinned food.

Clara Knowles, left, was employed as a beamer at Trencherfield Mill in the early 1950s, while right, the 'Under Carder' on duty on a Saturday morning about the same period poses in front of his machines.

Walking Tour

No.1 Wigan Pier, in the spring sunlight. Today the arched loading bays are home to the Heritage Centre's waterbuses and Kittiwake, *the Education Service's floating classroom.*

> **Cross the canal by the wooden bridge in front of the Terminal Warehouse, and turn left towards the Wigan Pier Shop.**

The next building – stone faced – was constructed in the 1790s, with the narrower (town) end being built just a few years later. So, by the year 1800, the eastern end of the Liverpool to Wigan canal was marked by these two elegant stone buildings. Unlike the Terminal Warehouse, there was no protection for the loading and unloading of barges, as the wooden canopied hoist was probably not added until the second half of the nineteenth century.

The canalside warehouses which house the shop, and beyond, the Orwell pub and restaurant.

Walking Tour

Work on the canal had originally started at both ends, and by 1774, it had extended eastwards from Liverpool only as far as Gathurst. The route from Gathurst to Wigan was, for the first few years, achieved by transferring to the Douglas Navigation – that part of the river which had been made navigable (from Wigan to the River Ribble) in 1742. The extension of the canal eastwards towards Wigan was only completed in the late 1770s. From the Leeds end, it had extended as far as Gargrave. At that point the money ran out and all work ceased. It would be another thirteen years before construction resumed. For many of those thirteen years, even the proposed route eastwards was open to change. It was not until 1816 that the canal as it exists today was completed. Until long after the canal was completed, the stone warehouse and the terminal warehouse stood alone alongside the Wigan Basin.

The brick warehouse which is attached to the 1790s stone warehouse, and which now houses the Orwell pub and restaurant, dates from a major expansion of warehousing facilities about 1880. At that time the canal was still at the heart of the freight network for the area, despite the opening of the railway from Wigan to Liverpool in 1848. In the mid-nineteenth century, goods were transported between Wigan and every one of the fifty-six towns along the canal's length.

Canal transport may have been slow, but it was very cost effective, and although revenues for the canal as a whole had started to drop almost as soon as the railway network started to be developed, some stretches of the canal were still seeing an increase in their trade. The Wigan to Liverpool stretch was just such a route, and with the bulk transportation of coal westwards and cotton eastwards, the boats were kept fully laden.

And the boats that travelled west from Wigan were more efficient carriers than those which travelled east. While the canal from Wigan to Liverpool was equipped with locks capable of taking the standard-size barge – 14ft 6in beam, 72ft length – the locks eastwards from Wigan were only capable of taking a 61ft 'short boat'.

While at first all the boats were rope-hauled by horses, barges were starting to be pulled by steam tugs as early as 1844/5 – steam coming to Wigan by water at least a year earlier than by rail! Steam did not take over at all quickly, however, and the complex system of towpaths and 'cross-over' bridges – which allowed the horses to be transferred from one towpath to the other without ever having to be disconnected from the boats – was well used until the closing years of the nineteenth century. Indeed, early twentieth-century photographs still show that horse-drawn boats were the rule rather than the exception. The size of the horses was enormous – but then so was the weight they had to pull. A fully laden 72ft barge could carry about 70 tons of coal!

Walking Tour

> *From the Orwell, walk across the courtyard to 'The Way We Were' exhibition in the 1890s warehouse.*

By the 1890s when the last warehouse was built, the idea of an extended canopy over the canal had been introduced. The warehouse was originally used for mixed goods, but predominantly cotton for much of its early life.

Inside it, from 1986 until 2007, was a remarkable recreation of living and working conditions in and around Wigan a century ago.

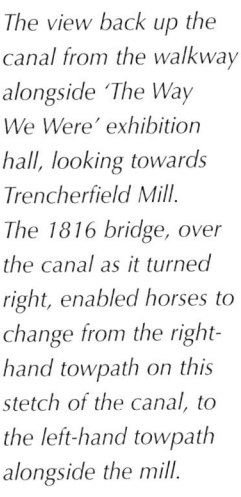

The late 1890s warehouse now houses 'The Way We Were' exhibition of what life was like in Wigan c.1900.

The view back up the canal from the walkway alongside 'The Way We Were' exhibition hall, looking towards Trencherfield Mill. The 1816 bridge, over the canal as it turned right, enabled horses to change from the right-hand towpath on this stetch of the canal, to the left-hand towpath alongside the mill.

Walking Tour

But Wigan Pier is as much a myth as it is a part of the town's history, so expect a seaside pier in this building as well!

The original Wigan Pier story is said to have originated amongst a group of miners returning from a day trip to Southport in 1891 – or so believed Robert Taylor, onetime station master of Wigan Wallgate station.

Their train was stopped at the Pagefield Signal box just outside the town, and from the carriage windows, they could see the elevated chain-driven railway that moved heavily laden coal trunks from Bankes's Colliery down to the 'tippler' by the canalside where the coal was tipped into barges.

What they could see across the flooded moss was not only the elevated railway, but a little wooden engine house at a dog-leg in its length - looking for all the world like a pavilion at the end of a seaside pier – and probably not unlike the pier at Southport where they had just spent the day. When one of the passengers asked where they were, 'Wigan Pier' was the reply. The idea of a pier so far inland, and in a town which was seen as the archetype of the 'dark satanic' mining and mill town was a genuinely original and amusing one. But the people of Wigan never thought so! Popularised in music halls up and down the land by George Formby Senior, Wigan Pier soon became more famous than the town whose name it bore.

All four of these important buildings may seem a little incongruous in the environment in which they sit today, but a century ago, the mills and factories they served were crowded around them. A couple of the old mill buildings survive and can still be seen in amongst the modern car showrooms and factory units behind the warehouses. A century ago, however, thousands of people worked within a few minutes walk of this stretch of the canal, and their working lives touched writers and artists alike. The eminent Victorian painter Eyre Crowe's canvas 'The Dinner Hour, Wigan' which hangs in Manchester City Art Gallery was painted less than a hundred yards away at Taylor's Mill, and it is said that the noise of clogs on cobbles down Wallgate to the mills each morning was little short of deafening. The eccentric Victorian Arthur Munby, who was fascinated – indeed obsessed – by working women, wrote in his diary in 1873:

> At 5.30 am I was awoken by the tramp of the factory girls. My window at the Royal Hotel [now the site of W.H. Smith] looks upon the Market Place. I got up, and saw the broad street busy with women and girls, and all clogshoon and most of them with shawls on their heads, all tramping to work in groups of two and three, and all talking broad Lancashire audibly. Hundreds of them; and hardly any men. The sun had not risen; it was dawn, and great rosy clouds were in the sky.

Walking Tour

Beyond the now-closed exhibition warehouse and the adjacent car park, a small garden area has been created and, at the far end, a typical small canalside crane stands near a 'Bantam' diesel tug boat.

In the history of canal traffic, the horse had slowly given way to steam, and eventually to diesel. Steam-powered barges, and later diesel powered craft, typically also towed a 'butty boat' – a powerless former horse-drawn barge. A powered barge with its 'butty boat' could, between them, transport over 120 tons of coal.

> **After leaving 'The Way We Were' exhibition, walk past the warehouse along the wooden walkway, and rejoin the canal towpath.**

The British Waterways Board introduced diesel tugs in the late 1950s, extending the lives of the former horse-drawn boats with no power of their own. At several points along the canal, tugs could be found pulling several butty boats so heavily laden with coal that they were almost flush with the waterline!

Nearby is a small crane, typical of the design used on wharfs along the length of the canal.

With today's traffic on the canal limited to pleasure craft and, around the Wigan basin, the waterbuses and the floating classroom *Kittiwake*, it is hard to imagine what the wharfs looked like crowded with freight barges loading and unloading, and the waters of the canal itself constantly churned by passing coal barges.

To see some barges once again tied up beneath the canopied hoists would be a delight.

The Bantam Tug XXV was a modification of a river-tug design made in Brentford, specifically adapted for canal use. They powered the barges on the Leeds to Liverpool Canal from the 1950s through to the cessation of bulk freight traffic on the canal in the late 1960s.

Walking Tour

The warehouse which now houses the 'The Way We Were' exhibition, as it looked in the 1950s with tarpaulin-covered barges lined up alongside.

Once past the tug, the canal turns sharp right under Seven Stars bridge, but our walk takes us back towards the town.

And so to Wigan Pier! Walking from Seven Stars Bridge back towards Trencherfield Mill, the hump of Wigan Pier is only a few yards ahead. The canal was once lined with 'coal tipplers' where the coal was loaded directly from railway wagons into the waiting barges. But why a pier? Well, one of the dictionary definitions of a pier describes it simply as an abutment of stone or wood used as a landing stage. In that respect, the canal was designed with many piers along its length, and this one was certainly known as Bankes's Pier by the 1880s. The coal tippler at Crooke, a few miles away, was described as a pier in the 1870s, so it is likely that many others were as well.

Walk towards Seven Stars Bridge, cross the bridge and return to the canal by the towpath on the opposite side of the waterway.

Bankes's Pier was at the end of a long tramway built in the 1820s to carry coal from Stone House Colliery in Goose Green to the canal. It was later extended to Winstanley No.4 Colliery, Winstanley No.3, and Clapgate.

Initially, the movement of the coal tubs along the tramway was by gravity alone, the track being laid with very carefully graded inclines, but after a number of mishaps, brake cars were added by the 1830s. By the 1870s steam locomotives were widely in use pulling six or eight trucks at a time. Each coal tub, as it arrived by the canalside, was rolled into the curved rails, and its cargo then tipped straight into the waiting barge.

As 'Wigan Pier' grew in fame, pleasure craft which had plied the canal for years changed the name of their starting point from Wigan Basin to

Walking Tour

Wigan Pier, and the name stuck even although the tippling pier itself was demolished in 1929 and sold for scrap.

But, like a phoenix rising from the ashes, fifty-five years after the original was sold, the replica pier was built by students at Wigan and Leigh College and installed in time for the Queen's visit to open the Heritage Centre.

Just past the pier, a former warehouse building from the late nineteenth century was converted into the 'Barge Inn' nightclub in the 1980s, but later became 'The Pier Nightspot'. Local people remember it as a warehouse when, on hot summer days, the apprentices who worked there would 'skinny-dip' in the canal at lunchtime.

A few yards further on, the canal turns sharp right under Pottery Road bridge, and starts its long journey towards Leeds. The towpath on the right was interrupted by Mayors' boatyard, so the horses pulling the barges had to move to the other side of the canal.

The towpath runs up a steeply cobbled slope, over the bridge and then, sharply turning back on itself, going back down and under the bridge span. This ingenious design means that the horse could change from one side of the canal to the other without needing to be disconnected from the barge it was pulling. In order to reduce wear on the tow ropes, wooden rollers were fitted to the bridge pillars. Eventually the rollers themselves were worn away by friction from the ropes, and all were replaced in the 1980s.

Wigan Pier floodlit at dusk in 1986 at the time of the Queen's visit to open the Heritage Centre. There were plans to replace this non-working replica with a fully operational tippler, but it was never done. In the original, a workman sat below the tippler just above water level working the tipping mechanism.

Walking Tour

The waterbus Emma *passes under the towpath bridge as it makes its way into the cutting by the side of Trencherfield Mill.*

Walking along the canal from the bridge, the open land on the opposite side was the site of Mayor's boatyard, from where countless barges were launched sideways into the canal, the splash they made covering the towpath in front of the mill.

> **Continue to walk along the towpath, alongside Trencherfield Mill towards the lock gates and the dry dock beyond.**

Just after Trencherfield Mill, a cutting runs underneath the bridge to give access to the mill's loading bay. In that cutting today is the waterbus terminus. The waterbus runs regularly from the mill to the 'The Way We Were' exhibition, and it is well worth the few minutes it takes to make the return trip and experience the world from water level.

Beyond the lock gate, beneath a typical late Victorian canopy, a small dry dock is still in regular use. Beyond that, the canal curves away around the town, before arriving at the impressive flight of locks which takes it high above the town and on its way towards Yorkshire.

Our walk takes us back past *Roland* and back round to the front of the mill to visit Opie's Museum of Memories.

Regular canal traffic across the Pennines ceased around 1960, and by 1964 almost all commercial traffic along the main cut had also ceased. Coal deliveries to Wigan's now-demolished Westwood Power Station in Poolstock ceased in the early 1970s, by which time the canal around Wigan Pier was at its most derelict. Twelve years of neglect was halted in the mid-1980s when the inspired restoration was begun, bringing us up

The towpath passes over Pottery Road Bridge allowing the horses to be moved from one side of the canal to the other.

Walking Tour

A giant fireplace adorned with ornaments marks the entrance to Opie's Museum of Memories, the only part of the site not directly related to the history of Wigan.

to date and to the end of our walk around the unique heritage site that is Wigan Pier.

In 1929 the *Wigan Observer* commenting on a report in the *Guardian* that Wigan Pier was to be dismantled, noted 'That is rather like announcing that four o'clock tomorrow afternoon is to be thoroughly overhauled and painted green! and asked What do they know of Wigan Pier who say it can be dismantled? You might as well ask about spring-cleaning a rainbow.' There can be few places which owe their appeal to, and have risen above, a century-old joke, but Wigan Pier – the myth and the reality – has always been unique.

The barge Viktoria *moored alongside the new Wigan Investment Centre, one of the enterprises which is bringing new life to the canalside. Beyond the barge, the canal makes its way up through a flight of 23 locks to Top Place, and north-eastwards towards the Pennines.*

Bibliography

Anderson, Donald, *Life and Times at Haigh Hall*, Smiths Books, 1991

Anderson, Donald and France, A.A., *Wigan Coal and Iron*, Smiths Books, 1994

Bilsborough, Norman, *The Treasures of Lancashire*, North West Civic Trust, 1989

Blakeman, Bob, *Wigan A Century Ago*, Landy Publishing, 1990

Burnett, Frances Hodgson, *That Lass O'Lowrie's*, Frederick Warne, 1877

Davies, Alan, and Hudson, Len, *The Wigan Coalfield*, Tempus, 1999

Defoe, Daniel, *A Tour through the Whole Island of Great Britain*, Penguin, 1986

Gillies, A. D. *Wigan Through Wickham's Window*, Philimore, 1986

Fairhurst, James, *Wigan's Worst Victorian Murders*, Book Clearance Centre, 2001

Grindon, Leo, *Lancashire – Brief Historical and Descriptive Notes*, Aurora Publishing, 1995

Hannavy, John, *Historic Wigan*, Carnegie, 1990

Hannavy, John, and Ryan, Chris, *Working in Wigan Mills*, Smiths Books, 1987

Hannavy, John, and Winstanley, Jack, *The Illustrated History of Wigan Pier*, Smiths Books, 1985

Hiley, Michael, *Victorian Working Women*, Gordon Fraser, 1979

Hill, Lawrence, *Gentlemen of Courage – Forward*, Magnolia Publishing, 1987

Holcroft, Fred, *The English Civil War Around Wigan and Leigh*, Wigan Heritage Service, 1993

Holcroft, Fred, *A Terrible Nightmare*, Wigan Heritage Service, 1992

Holcroft, Fred, *Murder, Terror and Revenge in Mediaeval Lancashire*, Wigan Heritage Service, 1992

Holcroft, Fred, *They Lived With Death*, Fred Holcroft, 1996

Miller, Garry, Historic *Houses in Lancashire: The Douglas Valley 1300-1700*, Heritage Trust for the North West, 2003

Orwell, George, *The Road to Wigan Pier*, Penguin, 2001

Sinclair, David, *The History of Wigan*, Thomas Wall, 1882

Spencer, Nathaniel, *The Complete English Traveller*, J. Cooke, 1771

Acknowledgements

No book is ever solely the work of the author, and this volume is no exception. I could not have produced it without the accumulated help of a great many people over the twenty-five years I have been writing about the town. As always, my sincere thanks go to Len Hudson, and Alistaor Gillies, former head of Heritage Services at the Wigan Leisure and Culture Trust, both for permission to use a number of images from the Wigan Heritage Service Collection, and for the quality of Len's excellent copy prints. Thanks also to Marilyn and David Parkinson for permission to use several of the fine images in their postcard collection, and to Alan Robinson for the chance to copy images from his family collection. Thanks also to Malc and Di Meadows for access to their wealth of material on the Boar's Head Inn. I am forever grateful to my co-authors on earlier projects – especially Chris Ryan and Jack Winstanley – who contributed greatly to my knowledge of Wigan's history – and for the generosity of local people, too many to mention over the years, in allowing me to copy their treasured photographs and build up the large collection of historic images I am able to draw on today. To all of them my sincere thanks. All the modern photography is my own.